For the Ones You Love

For the Ones You Love

JEREMY DRONFIELD
Illustrated by Raquel Lagartos

PUFFIN

PUFFIN BOOKS

UK | USA | Canada | Ireland | Australia
India | New Zealand | South Africa

Puffin Books is part of the Penguin Random House group of companies
whose addresses can be found at global.penguinrandomhouse.com

www.penguin.co.uk   www.puffin.co.uk   www.ladybird.co.uk

First published 2025

001

Text copyright © Jeremy Dronfield, 2025
Illustrations copyright © Raquel Lagartos, 2025
Photo on page 325 courtesy of Valerie Prestage and Lynn Reeves

The moral right of the author and illustrator has been asserted

Penguin Random House values and supports copyright.
Copyright fuels creativity, encourages diverse voices, promotes freedom
of expression and supports a vibrant culture. Thank you for purchasing
an authorized edition of this book and for respecting intellectual property
laws by not reproducing, scanning or distributing any part of it by any
means without permission. You are supporting authors and enabling
Penguin Random House to continue to publish books for everyone.
No part of this book may be used or reproduced in any manner for the
purpose of training artificial intelligence technologies or systems. In accordance
with Article 4(3) of the DSM Directive 2019/790, Penguin Random House
expressly reserves this work from the text and data mining exception.

Set in 10.75/17pt Sabon LT Std by
Six Red Marbles UK, Thetford, Norfolk
Printed and bound in Great Britain by Clays Ltd, Elcograf S.p.A.

The authorized representative in the EEA is Penguin Random House Ireland,
Morrison Chambers, 32 Nassau Street, Dublin D02 YH68

A CIP catalogue record for this book is available from the British Library

ISBN: 978–0–241–67551–9

All correspondence to:
Puffin Books
Penguin Random House Children's
One Embassy Gardens, 8 Viaduct Gardens, London SW11 7BW

Penguin Random House is committed to a
sustainable future for our business, our readers
and our planet. This book is made from Forest
Stewardship Council® certified paper.

For Val,
who told me the story
and without whom this book would not exist.

Contents

Introduction	ix
The First Day	1
A Four-Legged Chicken	19
A Proper *Schweinehund*	33
The Secret of the Crossings	51
A Bag of Beans	67
Zbaszyn	79
The Soldier	91
Going Home	103
Things That Happen in War	121
The District of Doomed Souls	131
Blackbirds and Morphine	145
A World Full of Sledgehammers	161
Don't Think. Don't Imagine.	183
The Camp	207
These Were Once People	229
The Pits of Turkheim	249

CONTENTS

Evacuation	269
The Second House	283
The Way Home	303
What Happened After	315
Acknowledgements	323

Introduction

Imagine if everything was taken away from you. All the things you own, the things you love, even the *people* you love. All taken away because someone who is powerful doesn't like your skin colour or the church you go to or the language you speak. You'd be sad, of course, and you'd be afraid. But maybe – just maybe – you'd discover other feelings. Perhaps a streak of bravery that you never knew you had. The courage to fight back, to live, to cherish and protect the little you had left.

This book tells a story about a time when that happened to millions of people all at once. It's a true story, even though at times it seems so incredible that you'd think it was made up.

True stories can be thrilling to read, but sometimes they can be hard. That's because they happened to real people, not made-up ones. Real people who were alive just like you are, and felt just as you do, who laughed when they were joyful and cried when they were sad.

People who loved their families and were loved in return.

But although the people in such stories suffered bad things, sometimes they found that they were strong and brave, and they survived. And perhaps that means that you can be strong and brave too.

The story I'm going to tell you is about two little girls who were like that. They were twin sisters. Their names were Friedel and Gina Rosenthal.* Their story happened many years ago, in a time long before you were born, probably before even your grandparents were born. But Friedel and Gina were every bit as real as you are. And when bad things happened, they found that they were stronger than they could ever have imagined. They discovered that they had courage.

Their story begins in the German city of Dusseldorf in the year 1930, when their lives were still good. We first meet them on a particular day in September; a big occasion for the twins because it was their very first day at school.

---

* Their names are pronounced *Freedel* and *Geena* (with a 'hard' G, as in 'girl').

CHAPTER ONE

The First Day

1930

In all the excitement about their first day at school, the twins had both put on the wrong coats.

The weather was chilly, so there were lots of clothes for Friedel and Gina to get themselves into. Their mum wanted them to make a good impression at school, but she had four other children besides Friedel and Gina. Although the family had a maid to help with the chores, only half of Mum's attention was on the twins.

Clothes for cold weather were thick and heavy in those days. Chunky sweaters were pulled down over Friedel and Gina's flowery dresses, then long woollen stockings that always went baggy and wrinkled at the knees. Then their stiff, bulky overcoats. On their heads they wore berets – Gina pulled hers down to her eyebrows to keep away the outdoor chill.

Friedel giggled. 'You look like a mushroom,' she said.

Mum helped them lace up their clunky ankle boots, then they hauled their leather satchels over their shoulders. She stood back to admire them.

Her face fell. 'You've put on each other's coats!'

The girls looked at one another. Friedel and Gina were twins, but like a lot of twins they weren't identical. Far from it. Gina was taller than Friedel by a couple of centimetres – which is quite a lot when you're six years old. Gina's dress stuck out below the hem of Friedel's coat. Meanwhile, Gina's coat reached Friedel's knees and the sleeves were down over her knuckles.

They were about to take off their satchels to swap coats, but Mum stopped them. 'You look adorable. We've got to take a photo. Come on.'

Mum shepherded the girls out of the apartment and down the stairs.

The Rosenthal family lived in a very nice apartment on the first floor of a small block. It was an old, handsome building. On the ground floor was their father's shop. It wasn't his only one – he owned two more in other parts of the city – but this one was home. It was a type of shop that Germans call a *Trinkhalle*. From it, you could buy sweets or tobacco or newspapers, as well as cakes, snacks and drinks – hot or cold – to take out.

Mum pushed Friedel and Gina in through the door at the back of the shop. They were welcomed by the familiar rich smells of pastry, caramel and hot coffee, all mixed in with the sharp aromas of tobacco and newspapers. Jars of coloured sweets stood in rows on the shelves – bon-bons, humbugs, rainbow sherbet, lollipops, lemon drops – every kind you could think of. Chocolate bars of every variety were displayed on the counter. Sweet buns and cream cakes were piled up under glass domes. To most children it was a dreamland of sugary delights, but to the Rosenthal kids it was simply home.

Mum called out, 'Hans! Get the camera. Come and take a picture of your sisters.'

Hans was fifteen years old, and the twins' eldest brother. He'd left school and now worked in the shop. (In those days in Germany, most children only went to school for eight years, and left when they were fourteen.) A handsome, dark-haired boy, Hans stood behind the counter each day measuring out sweets and tobacco, serving coffee, folding newspapers, and dreaming of running away to have an adventure.

Thankful for the distraction, Hans went upstairs to fetch the camera.

Their father was getting ready to go out and inspect the other shops, checking his bike and putting clips on his trouser bottoms.

'Abraham,' said Mum. 'Don't your daughters look nice for their first day?'

Their father turned and gazed down at them. He was a tall man with a long face that always wore a rather stern expression. Everything about him, from his hat to his bike clips, was neat and proper and *very* serious. 'Good morning, girls,' he said.

'Good morning, Father,' said Friedel and Gina, standing to attention.

He nodded. 'You appear suitably dressed. Very good.' He didn't seem to notice the coats.

Their older sister Martha came in from the apartment, also on her way to school. 'Are you two ready to go yet?' she asked as she buttoned up her coat.

Aged eleven, Martha walked awkwardly, with stiff legs and hunched shoulders. When she was much younger, she'd caught polio, a disease that can cause significant disability.* Martha had been lucky. Father had done everything in his power to help her recover. He'd taken her to lots of different doctors, which was expensive, and spent hours helping her with exercises to make her arms and legs work again. In those days, most people who lived in cities didn't own cars unless they were rich or needed them for their work, but Father

---

* Polio doesn't exist in Europe now because of vaccination. But in the time when this story took place it was quite common.

bought a motorbike with a sidecar just so that he could take Martha to different doctors. His efforts had paid off. Despite starting out almost completely paralysed, Martha could walk and get about as other children did. She couldn't run or raise her arms very far, but she was happy.

'Good morning, Father,' she said.

'Good morning, Martha dear.' Father gave one of his rare smiles. Martha was very much his favourite. Sometimes she worried that her brothers and sisters were jealous, but of course they weren't. Martha was so sweet it was impossible to have bad feelings about her.

Hans came back with the camera, and they went outside. The shop stood at the corner of Marken Street and Hildener Street. As usual, it was a bustle of traffic and pedestrians. Lorry engines roared and horse-drawn carts rattled along. There was a garage workshop next door, and the clink, clank and grind of mechanics' tools poured out of it into the general noise.

Friedel and Gina stood grinning while their picture was taken. In those days, cameras were much less common, and taking a photo was a bit of an occasion. Martha waited, sighing and tapping her foot. The twins were going to the same school as her, and as it was a long walk through busy city streets, Martha had to take them. She couldn't walk very fast, so they needed to set out in good time.

THE FIRST DAY

After Mum had waved her three daughters off, she went back inside and found Father still getting his bike ready.

'Did you remember the cigar order for the Bilk shop?' he asked. Bilk was a district of Dusseldorf, next to the district of Oberbilk, where Marken Street was. The Rosenthals' second shop was in Bilk, and the third was in the city centre, near the railway station. Father's tours of inspection each day involved a lot of pedalling.

'Of course,' she said. Mum was in charge of ordering stock for all three shops, and she had a busy day ahead of her, on top of looking after the younger kids. 'Make sure you check their pipe tobacco, won't you, Abraham?'

He frowned. 'You know I asked you not to call me by that name any more, Helene. At least not in the shop. My name is now Adolf.'

She shuddered. 'I know, but I still don't understand why. That's such a horrid name.'

'For business, Helene, I prefer people not to realise we are Jewish.'

This was a sensitive subject for Mr Rosenthal. Jewish people have their own religion, with different beliefs about God. They have their own places of worship, called synagogues, and lots of special traditions. But in every other way they are just like anyone else. And yet, throughout history, people have been prejudiced against Jews. In Germany, since the beginning of the 1900s the prejudice had grown into a new kind of hatred. It had become especially bad since the end of the First World War, in 1918. Germany had lost, and some people had spread a false belief that it was the Jews' fault.

Those same people blamed Jews for just about everything that was wrong in the world, and for all of Germany's troubles. If people couldn't get jobs, or if families were poor – blame the Jews. Many people said that Jews were not proper Germans, and that they were a danger to the German way of life.

It was all complete nonsense. Nasty, vicious nonsense. Most Jews were just ordinary folk who simply wanted to live their lives, work at their jobs, do their shopping, raise their children, watch movies, listen to music, read books, go on holiday. All the normal things. Some Jews were extraordinary – famous artists and scientists. One of the greatest German scientists of that time, Albert Einstein, was Jewish. But more and more Germans believed the lies about them. People love to be able to point their finger and blame all their woes on *those people over there who are different from us*. Sometimes the thing that makes 'those people' different is their skin colour or their religion, sometimes their gender, sometimes the fact they're foreign. Fear and dislike of Jewish people is so common that there is a special word for it: *antisemitism*.

For the Rosenthal family, it was even more difficult, because they were not only Jewish but immigrants as well. Mum and Father – Helene and Abraham – were from Poland. Their eldest children, Hans and Martha, were born there. Then, when Martha was only a year old, there had been a terrible outbreak of antisemitism in their town, with awful violence against Jewish people. To escape from it, the Rosenthals moved to Germany and settled in Dusseldorf. There was antisemitism here too, but at the time it hadn't seemed as bad as it was in Poland.

And then the Nazis appeared.

The Nazis started out as a small group of people who wanted to change Germany. The disaster of losing the First World War plunged the country into chaos. Poverty was everywhere. The Nazis were extremely angry about this and wanted to make Germany great and mighty again. Not like it had been before the war, but better. The Nazis believed that Germany had once had a golden age, many years ago. It wasn't really true, but it became their dream to bring it back. Although they liked a lot of science and technology, they hated many other things about the modern world – strange modern art, women having careers, growing tolerance for gay people and other minorities. The list went on and on, and the Nazis blamed almost all of it on the Jews. Their antisemitism was a new, fiercer kind of antisemitism than anything Germany had seen before.

Nazism grew and grew in Germany during the 1920s, spreading across the country. Nazis began winning local elections, and by 1930, as Friedel and Gina were about to start school and their parents were working hard running their shops, Nazis were even gaining seats in the German parliament. They were now starting to believe that they would become the next government. The Nazis weren't nearly as popular in Dusseldorf as in some other parts of the country, but it was enough to make Jewish people feel very nervous.

Trying to fit in with German life, Mr and Mrs Rosenthal had given their children traditional German names instead of Jewish ones. Mr Rosenthal now believed that, in his business dealings, he needed to use a more German-sounding name himself. After trying out a few different ones, he had stopped using his Jewish given name of *Abraham*, and had started calling himself *Adolf*.

'But why *that* name?' said Mum as her husband wheeled his bike out of the door. 'The name of a Nazi, for goodness sake! *The* Nazi!'

It really was a strange choice for a Jewish man to make. 'Adolf' had once been a perfectly respectable German name, and there were many middle-aged men called Adolf about. But with the rise of the Nazis, it was now unbreakably linked to their leader, Adolf Hitler.

Mr Rosenthal didn't answer. Who knew what went on in his head? Many Jewish businessmen took on German-sounding names. They feared that some people might not buy from Jews or that banks might refuse to lend their businesses money. Perhaps Mr Rosenthal figured that if he didn't want to appear Jewish, it was safest to take the name of the man who hated Jews more than anyone. Or maybe he just liked the name and wanted to reclaim it for non-Nazis.

Mum watched him get on his bike and pedal off down Marken Street. She sighed and turned back to the warm, sweet-smelling welcome of the shop.

* * *

Martha said goodbye to her sisters at the school entrance, heading inside to meet up with her friends.

Standing on the pavement, Friedel and Gina looked up at the school in fear and wonder. It was a looming three-storey building with fancy brickwork and tall arched windows. It was enough to make any child feel very tiny indeed; a huge red-brick monster that could snap you up and swallow you in a single gulp. Who could tell what fearsome things might go on inside, what terrors might lurk there? Still, Martha went in every day and came out again alive and well, so it couldn't be too bad.

Gathering their courage and holding hands for safety, Friedel and Gina walked in through the big doors.

The entrance hall was bustling with kids, some even older than Martha. There was a big Christian cross on the wall, and a painting of a bearded man with light round his head. Friedel and Gina had no idea who he was, but he was clearly important. They learned later that this was

Jesus, and that Christians believed he was the son of God. Jews don't make pictures of God – they call it idolatry, and it's forbidden.

A friendly woman noticed the girls standing alone and bewildered by the door and asked them their names. She checked a list. 'Ah, you're in Mrs Schmidt's class,' she said. After helping them to put their coats in the cloakroom, she led them to their classroom.

It was in a big, strange room. Below the arched windows, blackboards lined the walls on all sides. There were orderly rows of desks, all facing the front of the room. Each desk had a wooden bench fixed to it, with room for two children. About thirty kids, boys and girls, were already there.

Mrs Schmidt greeted Friedel and Gina and told them to sit. They found a desk together. Its surface was battered and scratched from all the children who'd been here before them.

On the wall at the front of the class, where Mrs Schmidt had her desk, was another picture of Jesus, and a small statue of a sad-looking lady in a blue robe. This, the twins would learn, was Jesus's mum. She was called the Virgin Mary. On the wall above was a small cross with a tiny Jesus on it, his hands cruelly nailed to the crossbar. According to the stories, that was how he was killed. No wonder his mum looked sad.

So the day began – the first of many. There were lessons in maths, reading and writing, and from time to time stories about Jesus. The children each had a book called a primer, which had simple lessons and writing exercises to copy. Instead of paper, each child had a rectangle of slate, on which they wrote with chalk. They learned to read and write letters and numbers by repeating and practising them over and over and over again. Talking was forbidden. Mrs Schmidt spoke, and the children listened in silence. They were only allowed to speak when they were asked a question.

At lunchtime, Friedel and Gina sat in the yard at the back of the school and ate the sandwiches Mum had packed for them, feeling very lost. They were glad that they had each other. This was nothing like the Jewish kindergarten they'd been to last year, which had been a nice, friendly, fun place. The twins had been happy there.

Back in the classroom, Friedel noticed a few of the kids staring at her and Gina, and whispering to each other. She heard a girl mutter to a friend: *Jews*. The friend said something nasty in reply. How did they know?

Friedel found out later that there were only a few other Jewish kids in the class. It was a Catholic school, so of course most of the kids were from Catholic families. Somehow word had got around about who the Jewish kids were.

At the end of the day the twins met Martha at the entrance and began the long, weary walk home. It was about two and a half kilometres, and after a day

like the one they'd had it felt like a trek to the ends of the earth.

On the way home, they learned another important lesson about the world they lived in.

Walking along one of the main streets, they passed a group of older boys, some about Martha's age, some as old as Hans. They wore brown uniforms with shiny boots. On their sleeves were red armbands with the crooked cross symbol of the Nazis. It was called a *swastika*.

These boys were members of the Hitler Youth. In some ways it was a bit like Scouts, but the boys and girls were taught to believe in Nazi ideas – including hating Jews. The boys wore military-style uniforms and were being groomed to be Nazi soldiers when they grew up. The girls had their own section of the Hitler Youth, called the League of German Girls. They were expected to become traditional wives and mothers, and were trained to be fit and healthy and loyal to the Nazi cause.

Standing with the Hitler Youth boys were some grown-up men in similar uniforms – shiny boots, dark brown trousers, and a light brown shirt with a leather belt, an army-style cap and swastika armband. The men were known as Brownshirts, although they called themselves 'storm troopers'. They were the Nazi Party's thugs. Armed with batons, whenever they weren't guarding

Nazi meetings, they went around picking on Jews and anyone they didn't like the look of. The Hitler Youth boys often acted as junior storm troopers.

It looked as if they were organising one of their regular parades. Nazis loved to parade with their swastika flags and uniforms. It seemed to make them feel powerful. They were looking extremely proud of themselves and calling out slogans at people passing by – mostly about how much they wanted to get rid of Jews. Martha guided the twins across the road to avoid them. It wasn't safe to be noticed in the street by the Brownshirts.

The sisters arrived back in Marken Street just as Father was setting out on his evening round. At the end of every day he cycled to each of the shops to collect the money they'd taken. As he greeted the girls, Friedel and Gina looked close to tears.

'You are upset,' he said. 'What happened?'

'We saw Nazis,' said Martha. 'They were saying horrible things.'

Friedel spoke up. 'Kids at school said *dirty Jews*.'

Father frowned. 'Come inside,' he said. Leaning his bike against the shop window he led them indoors. Going behind the counter, he picked out a small chocolate bar and handed it down to Friedel. For Gina he picked a paper cone from the stack and scooped in some of her favourite sweets.

'There,' he said. 'Now enjoy those and forget the nasty people.'

As they tucked in, the worries of the day evaporated in a sweet rush of joy. But the chocolate and candies couldn't make those worries go away completely. They stayed there, like little bruises in the girls' minds.

CHAPTER TWO

A Four-Legged Chicken

1933

Friedel tried to keep her eyes focused on her book, but the words and pictures kept on drifting away from her. It was a Sunday afternoon and she was tired – not in the mood to learn the history of some crusty old king and his boring old war.

More than two years had passed since that first day at school. It hadn't got any better. In fact it was getting worse. The nasty comments from other kids came more often, and were spoken out loud rather than muttered. 'Dirty Jew' was the name she and Gina were usually called.

The Nazi poison was getting into so many people's thoughts now. Even some of the teachers joined in, making mean comments to the Jewish kids and sending them out of class for no reason. Mrs Schmidt was the only nice teacher. It upset her to see the bullying, but she didn't do anything about it. It was as if she was as scared of the other teachers as the Jewish kids were.

In the city streets, the Brownshirts and Hitler Youth were getting even more full of themselves. Home was one of the few safe places to be. Even that wasn't as good as it used to be. The family didn't live over the shop in Marken Street any more. They had moved to the other side of the city, to an apartment in Bright Road. The comforting smells and liveliness of the shop were no longer part of their daily life.

There were some good things about Bright Road. The walk to school was a lot shorter now. Also, it was only a little way to the Grafenberger Forest, a magical place of winding lanes and sunny glades where deer grazed. The whole family loved to go there for picnics and games in the summer, and sledging in the winter. In nice weather Father would cycle along the lanes with the kids, stopping now and then to pick wild fruits from the bushes. It felt like a whole different world. There were no Brownshirts there, and nobody called you bad names.

Friedel was desperate for summer to return. It was late January, and the bedroom was freezing cold. She yawned and put down her school book. She longed for the warmth of the living room, but Father was listening to opera on the radio, and nobody was allowed to make a sound.

There was a rush of footsteps outside the bedroom door and, grateful for the distraction, Friedel went out to the hall. Gina was just arriving home with their brother Bernard. Gina preferred the company of boys now. Although Bernard was aged ten, two years older than the twins, Gina spent most of her free time playing out with him and his friends.

The swirling, wailing sounds of opera music came through the closed living room door. Gina knocked on it. In German families in those days, children had to knock before entering a room where their parents were, especially if the parents were strict. Mr Rosenthal was especially fussy about such things.

'Come in,' said Mum's voice.

Gina, Bernard and Friedel entered the room, treading softly so as not to break Father's concentration. He sat in his favourite armchair, swallowed up in the mysterious, off-putting music he loved so much. Gina could never understand why he liked it – she thought the women's screeching sounded as if they were being tortured.

Their two oldest brothers were there. Hans sat reading a Polish newspaper. He was seventeen now, and almost a grown-up in his own right. Father had put him in charge of the Marken Street shop, but Hans's dreams of adventure had only become stronger as he grew older. He wanted to go back to Poland, the land where he'd been born, and join the army. Hans was determined and wilful, and there was every chance that he might just run away and do it.

Max was the middle brother – a year younger than Martha, and two years older than Bernard. He would be turning thirteen this year. That meant he would soon be ready for his bar mitzvah. The bar mitzvah is a very serious step for Jewish boys.* They study the Jewish religion in preparation for a solemn ceremony in which they are seen as becoming grown-ups in the eyes of God.

Father and Mum didn't bother much with their religion. Father considered himself what he called a 'free thinker', which meant he liked to make up his own mind about such things, rather than following what rabbis† or priests said. He encouraged the children to follow his ideas. But the family still held to some of their Jewish traditions, including bar mitzvahs for the boys. Many Jewish people do the same, even if they don't believe in the religion – just like people who celebrate Christmas and Easter and take the day off on Sunday even if they don't follow the Christian religion.

Of all the children, Max took his Jewishness most seriously. He had been attending a special Jewish school

---

* Girls have an equivalent called a bat mitzvah when they are either twelve or thirteen, although that is a more modern thing. Bat mitzvahs for girls were much less common in the 1930s.
† A rabbi is a Jewish priest. The word is pronounced as *rab-eye*.

called a *cheder** and was well prepared for his bar mitzvah.

At last, the opera wailed and trumpeted itself to an end, and the evening news began.

Mum and Father were visibly anxious as soon as it started. They were always anxious these days, because the news was always scary. Adolf Hitler and his Nazis were getting very close to being in power. This evening, the news was worse than ever.

The big wooden radio vibrated with the newsreader's sharp, urgent voice: 'Following the resignation of Chancellor Schleicher yesterday, discussions are under way in Berlin to decide on the appointment of a new chancellor.' In Germany, the chancellor is the leader of the country, like a prime minister, so this was very important news. People across the country were becoming more and more angry at the government, and they wanted change. As a result, Chancellor Schleicher had been forced out. But many people feared that the situation would give the Nazis a chance to gain real power.

Father gripped the arms of his chair, his knuckles turning pale. Hans sat forward, listening intently as the newsreader went on. They guessed what was coming next.

---

* This is said a bit like *hedder*. In Hebrew (the main Jewish language), *ch* is spoken in the same way as in languages like Welsh and German. You press the back of your tongue against the roof of your mouth and huff.

The voice from the radio continued: 'It is expected that the president will ask Mr Hitler to step into the role of chancellor . . .'

It droned on, but the Rosenthal family barely heard it. They sat stunned. It was the worst possible news. Jews everywhere had been dreading this happening. Adolf Hitler, the leader of the Nazi party, was going to be chancellor. The Jew-haters were closing their grip on Germany.

'That doesn't mean Hitler gets his way, though, does it?' said Hans. 'He can't hurt us, can he?'

Father shook his head. 'No, it won't be a Nazi government. They don't have enough members of parliament for that. There will be ministers from the other parties running the country. But Hitler will be in charge.'

Max's gaze flicked back and forth between Hans and their father. He looked as if he understood what they were talking about, but to Bernard, Friedel and Gina it all sounded like gibberish. They did sense one thing clearly, though – although their parents tried to hide it, they were scared. The twins had never seen such a thing. Grown-ups weren't supposed to be frightened of anything.

* * *

The last days of January and February trickled away with the melting ice. There was still a lot to enjoy in life. There were long weekend walks to the Grafenberger Forest – hauling the heavy sledge, swooshing down the wooded slopes with shrieks of joy, throwing snowballs, then the trek home again to Bright Road for supper in the toasty-warm comfort of the apartment.

But happiness was an illusion. Winter was leaving, making way for a monstrous spring.

A little over a month after that scary news programme, an election was held in Germany. It would decide whether Hitler would gain more power or not. If the Nazi Party won the election, they would have complete control of the government. At the last election, they'd won more votes than any other party, but not more than all the other parties put together. That was why they weren't in complete power. This new election might give them everything they wanted.

The Nazis were confident. Their supporters – especially the Brownshirt storm troopers – took to the streets to try to ensure victory. If they couldn't persuade enough Germans to vote for the Nazis, they planned to frighten them into it, or at least make them too scared to go out and vote for anyone else.

On the Friday before the election, Friedel, Gina and Martha walked home through the city streets. Brownshirt storm troopers and boys from the Hitler Youth were everywhere. They shouted out Nazi slogans and intimidated people. Lately they hadn't been picking

on Jews quite so much. Their targets for the moment were the other political parties: the Communist and Socialist parties. They were strong in Dusseldorf, and the Nazis were determined to stop them from campaigning, to try to win votes.

When the sisters arrived home, they found the apartment in uproar, and Mum and Father in a state. Mum was anxious and Father was downright angry. It had nothing to do with the Nazis or the elections. It was Hans. He'd finally followed his daydreams.

'He's gone,' said Mum.

'Gone? Where?' said Martha.

'Goodness knows. Your father went to check on the shop and Hans wasn't there. His passport is gone too.'

'He did not even lock the door. And he took all the money from the till. Every last penny.'

'How much was it?' asked Mum.

'How would I know?' said Father crossly. 'I didn't get to count it! Enough to take him to Poland, I should think. You know how the boy dreams. Foolish child!'

That evening, dinner was quieter and more tense than usual. It was Shabbos, a holy time for Jewish people that happens every week. It begins at sunset on Friday and ends at sunset on Saturday. On Friday, most Jews have Shabbos dinner, which is special in the same way as Sunday lunch is for many non-Jewish people.

After the candles had been lit to mark the beginning of Shabbos, the Rosenthals sat down at the dining table. On one side, Friedel, Gina and Martha, and at each end, Mum and Father. On the other side, Max, Bernard and a very conspicuous empty chair where Hans should have been. The table was laden with dishes. Mum served it all in silence. There was gefilte fish, which is a kind of pâté made from white fish. Then there came the children's favourite, lokshen soup (chicken noodle), and a main meal of chicken to follow.

At one end of the table, Father had his own dinner. He was a strict vegetarian. He often tried to encourage the children to do likewise, but they loved their lokshen soup too much. And so he sat alone with his meat-free meal.

Gina was always a bit puzzled by the chicken. It was served in pieces in a dish, with wings and legs. There were always four legs, because that was how Mum bought them. Gina had never seen a real-live chicken – or a whole cooked one – and she imagined they must be the most peculiar birds, with four legs like a cat or a dog. But this evening her mind was more distracted by the harmonica in her pocket. She'd begun learning to play, and was itching to go to her room and practise.

Friedel always felt a bit of dread as the end of dinner approached. With seven people, there were lots of dirty plates, dishes and cutlery, and all the girls were expected to help Mum clear the table and wash up. Friedel hated it. The moment came when the last morsel had been eaten and Father had drained the last sip of wine from his glass. Friedel watched with eagle eyes for the signal that clearing up was about to start ...

Mum moved her chair back, ready to stand.

Friedel jumped up. 'Just going to the toilet,' she said. And before Mum could say anything, Friedel was out of the door.

Gina and Martha were better behaved. Without complaint, they gathered up the dishes and carried them out to the kitchen. Minutes went by, and Friedel still didn't come back. Gina could sense Father's temper rising. Friedel usually got away with it, but this evening Father just wasn't in the mood.

In the bathroom, Friedel sat on the edge of the bath, finding refuge in the private world of her own thoughts. With one ear she listened out for the sounds of the washing-up coming to an end. Instead, she heard the sudden banging of knuckles on the bathroom door, and Father's cross voice.

'Friedel! Come out of there at once!' Nervously she unlocked the door. It opened to reveal Father glowering down at her. 'This is quite enough, young lady. Now go to the kitchen and help your mother and your sisters.'

There was no question of disobeying Father. Crestfallen and miserable, Friedel did as she was told.

As she walked away, Father added, a bit more kindly, 'Every person must do their duty, Friedel. If every person helps, then life is less hard for everyone – including you. You will learn the lesson one day.'

* * *

The Nazis didn't win the election. At least, not quite. They gained a lot more votes than they ever had before, and won new seats in parliament. But although they still didn't have a complete majority, they were more powerful than before. They also formed an alliance with other politicians in parliament who shared some of their views, meaning that Hitler was bound to feel bolder now.

And so it turned out. Less than three weeks after the election, Hitler seized complete power for himself. He did it by persuading the president to help him pass a law that made him the absolute leader of Germany. Presidents had very little power in Germany (not like in America). Besides, President Hindenburg approved of Hitler. The law was passed, and Hitler took total control of the government. He had always been known as the *Führer* ('Leader') in the Nazi Party, with complete authority over everyone in it. Now he became Führer of the whole nation. Germany had officially become *Nazi* Germany.

In the Rosenthal home, Mum and Father talked about it often, in nervous tones. Max took a close interest too. They told one another that the Nazis wouldn't do anything bad to the Jewish people. Not really. After all, Hitler was surrounded by more sensible people who weren't Nazis – such as those who had arranged for him to become chancellor. They would make sure that he and his ministers behaved like a normal government in charge of a country.

Unfortunately, this consoling idea would turn out to be every bit as fanciful as Gina's belief in four-legged chickens.

At least there was one happy event for the Rosenthals. Hans came home. He had indeed gone to Poland, in the hope of joining the army. His passport visa had expired, though, and his money had run out. The Polish police arrested him and sent him back to Germany. But although he'd returned home and gone back to work, Hans hadn't given up his dreams. He'd tasted adventure in Poland, the land of his birth, and he wanted more.

CHAPTER THREE

A Proper *Schweinehund*

1937

'Maybe it'll be nice,' said Gina.

'I doubt it,' said Friedel. 'How can a coal yard be nice?'

'Wait and see,' said Mum, shifting the weight of her heavy suitcase from one hand to the other. 'Whether it's nice or not, it's the best we can do, and it was very generous of Mr Wallach to offer it to us.'

If Bernard had an opinion, he kept it to himself. His suitcase was hurting his hand so much it felt like it was on fire. They had walked endless kilometres through the Dusseldorf streets, carrying most of their belongings with them. They were on their way to a new home.

Four years had gone by since Hitler came to power, and life for Jewish people had got worse and worse. Father had lost all but one of his shops. Jews were still allowed to work and own shops and other businesses, but the local governments were filled with Nazis now. They did all they could to make life difficult for Jewish businesses. Also, the Brownshirts encouraged people to avoid buying from Jews. Father had struggled to keep the shops open, but it was hard. Takings from customers were less. On top of that, Mum had a difficult time getting stock that was affordable, and the rents on the shops were expensive. So now there was just one left.

Even that was hard to run when people called you 'dirty Jew' and neighbours who'd been good friends before turned their backs on you. One morning Father had arrived at the shop to open up and found a bullet hole in the door. The bullet had gone right through and hit the back wall behind the counter. He guessed that some Nazi must have thought he might be in there counting the takings.

There was often violence against Jews, and against anyone who stood up to the Nazis. One of the Rosenthals' neighbours, a kind man called Mr Junkermann, refused to give the Nazi salute when a parade of Hitler Youth passed along Bright Road. The Brownshirts pounced on him and beat him almost unconscious. Mr Junkermann wasn't Jewish, but he was loyal to his Jewish friends – his daughter was a close friend of Martha.

The constant fear and the loss of the shops was bad enough. Now even the Rosenthals' home had been taken away from them. The man who owned the apartment building had told Father that he couldn't have Jews living in his property any more. They had to move out. For a short while they'd been allowed to stay in a little apartment above a tailor's shop in the city centre. And now they were having to move yet again, trekking with all their belongings across the city.

This wasn't the life that Friedel and Gina had been born into, but kids are very good at getting used to things. The family was smaller than it had been. Hans, who was now a proper grown-up, had finally gone off to live in Poland. There, he'd fulfilled his dream of joining the Polish army. Max too had left home, even though he was still only seventeen. He was working in a Jewish farming community near the city of Berlin. He was hoping to go and live on a special kind of farm called a *kibbutz* in Palestine, a place that many Jews all over the world regarded as their true homeland.*

---

* The nation of Israel didn't officially exist in 1937. The region was then known as the 'Palestine territory', or the British Mandate for Palestine (because it was run by the British government). Part of it became the country of Israel in 1948.

Even without the older boys, the apartment above the tailor's had been small for six people. The place they were going to now was bigger, but probably not better.

It had been offered to them by a Jewish friend of Father's called Max Wallach. Mr Wallach was a coal seller – a profitable business in those days when most people's houses were heated by coal fires. Mr Wallach also owned a small apartment building. The apartments were all full, but at the back of the building was the place where he ran his coal business. Because Mr Wallach was Jewish, his trade had gone bad just like Father's had. His office was unused, and he'd offered it to the Rosenthals to live in. They were desperate for a roof over their heads, so Father and Mum had accepted gratefully.

'This way,' said Father as they turned a corner. He was wheeling his bike with one hand and carrying a suitcase in the other. 'Wallach's place is in Germania Street.'

They were in the Bilk district, not far from Father's last remaining shop. This was the western half of Dusseldorf, near the docks, a long way from the peace of the Grafenberger Forest. They walked under the dripping gloom of a big railway bridge just as a train thundered over it, pouring out steam, smoke and cinders. On the other side, they found themselves in a long street. It

was lined with small, rather plain shops and apartment buildings, just like most of the streets they'd traipsed through on the way here.

Father led them to number 28, a four-storey building with an arched passageway leading to the back. It didn't look at all inviting, and the kids stared at it glumly. The Rosenthals went through the dark, dusty passage and found themselves in a big yard behind the building.

If anything, the yard was even less pleasant than the passageway. It was all coal, coal, and more coal. Great heaps of it between roofless wooden walls that were stained black. The ground was dark with coal dust, and the air reeked of it.

The family gazed at the place in dismay. Friedel had been right. It really wasn't nice.

'We're not living in this, are we?' said Bernard.

'Not in the *yard*, silly,' said Martha. 'We're living in the office.'

Off to one side was a building joined to the back of the apartments. It had dusty windows and a coal-blackened iron staircase leading up to the door.

Mum pointed. 'That'll be it, I expect.'

While Father went off to find Mr Wallach, Bernard, Friedel, Gina and Martha looked at each other. None of them spoke, but their expressions all said *uh-oh*.

Father came back with Mr Wallach, a kindly man who welcomed them, flourished a bunch of keys and led them up the steps. The iron treads clanged forbiddingly under their boots.

Inside was a little hallway, then a long, dim corridor with three rooms leading off it. They contained some rather worn office furniture, filing cabinets, stacks of bills and receipts, all gathering dust. It had once been a hive of bustle and money-making, but that was over now. The whole place had a depressing air of neglect and bleakness.

While Mr Wallach showed Mum and Father around, Bernard and the girls explored the rooms. It wasn't quite as bad as they'd feared. But then the girls thought back to their old home in Marken Street. It had felt quite ordinary at the time, comfortable and warm. In their memories now, that apartment above the sweet-smelling *Trinkhalle* seemed like a luxurious mansion. Even the plainer apartment in Bright Road had at least been pleasant.

The family made the best they could of the office-apartment. It was agreed that Martha, Friedel and Gina would share the first room, Bernard could sleep in the middle room – which would also serve as the living room and kitchen – and Mum and Father would have the room at the end. They managed to buy or borrow some cheap, simple beds, and Mum and the girls set about airing and cleaning the place (with an eye on Friedel, making sure she didn't skulk off to avoid the chores). Once they'd unpacked their belongings and made the beds, it felt a bit better. Not nice, but more like somewhere they could bear to live.

Although the coal yard was close to Father's shop, Germania Street was a very long way from everywhere else, including Martha's work. Martha, who was now eighteen, had left school four years ago. She had a sewing job with a Jewish woman named Mrs Boehrer, who made fine underwear for rich women.

Friedel and Gina, still aged thirteen, should have had another year left in school. But Jewish kids weren't welcome any more, so they'd had to leave. Also, the family needed whatever money they could earn. Mrs Boehrer, knowing their desperate situation, and being fond of Martha, had agreed to take the twins into her sewing workshop and teach them.

* * *

'Well, I dare say all our lives have changed, and not for the better,' said Mrs Boehrer, pouring coffee into the girls' cups.

Martha, Friedel and Gina were sitting at the dining table in Mrs Boehrer's private room in the basement below the shop. They'd just finished lunch. Their empty plates lay before them, wiped clean by the hungry girls. Mrs Boehrer knew how bad things had become for the Rosenthals, and always took care to give the sisters a good meal. With them sat Rosa, the other girl who helped with the sewing. On the other side of the table were Mrs Boehrer's two grown-up sons, who ran the money side of the business.

'That Hitler will ruin everything before he's finished,' Mrs Boehrer went on, putting down the coffee pot. 'I don't know what will become of us.' She shook her head sadly. 'So upsetting.'

Mrs Boehrer had managed to keep her business thriving because it was completely private. She didn't advertise. The women for whom she made underwear got to know her through their friends, and only came to the shop by appointment. They were all rich and liked the private service, so they were happy to keep quiet about it being a Jewish-owned business. And since Mrs Boehrer had lots of money herself and owned her own premises, she could mostly avoid the attention of the authorities.

After they'd finished their coffee, they went back to work. The sons went through to their office, with its rows of neat cash books, order books and filing cabinets, while Mrs Boehrer and her young women trooped upstairs to the shop.

It wasn't a typical shop – there was no counter or cash register, and no big display windows or signs. If you were a suitable client you would know where it was, and if you weren't, you wouldn't be welcome. So the shop looked more like a fashionable sitting room, with comfortable, stylish furniture for the clients. Samples of ladies' underwear were on display, all tasteful and beautifully made.

When a client came in, Mrs Boehrer would greet them and chat, serve them tea or coffee from fine china cups, discuss designs, and take the client's measurements.

The making and stitching was done in the workshop at the back of the building. There were work benches with sewing machines and a big cutting table for snipping out the fabric from the paper patterns. Around the walls were shelves piled with huge rolls of silk and satin, gauze and cotton, in every colour you could think of – rose pink, ivory, lilac, sky blue, mint green ... There were ribbons and lace in matching shades, rolls of elastic, and reels upon reels of silk thread.

This was where Martha and Rosa worked, making the garments. All day long they toiled, slicing through sheets of silk with heavy steel scissors, or sitting with heads bowed as they worked with their needles, or feeding fabric through chattering sewing machines.

Martha was proud of her work. It was far better than being in a noisy, dirty factory, and she liked how posh it all was. Now she was helping to teach her younger sisters the same skills.

Today they were learning how to stitch together a bra. It was extremely complicated, with so many different pieces that fitted together in mind-bending ways. Both the twins took to sewing quite well, especially Gina, who delighted in stitching the soft silk straps. She soon began to pick up the knack of getting the stitches small and neat, although the tricky parts of the bra were well beyond both the girls. They hoped one day they'd be able to make some of these beautiful things for themselves.

* * *

It was a long working day at Mrs Boehrer's, six days a week. Although it wasn't arduous labour, it was tiring. Stooping and concentrating on fiddly tasks for hours at a time left you with a stiff neck and sore eyes. The girls' fingers were dotted red where the needle had pricked them.

At the end of each weary day, the three sisters faced the long walk home. Mrs Boehrer's shop was on the opposite side of the city from Germania Street. Jewish workers couldn't take the bus, so the girls had to walk the whole way. It took nearly an hour.

One Saturday at the beginning of October, they left the shop at four o'clock – a little early. It had been a quiet day, with not much work to do. Outside, the streets were buzzing with activity. There were far more people around than usual and there was a sense of excitement in the air. The girls knew what was going on. It had been in the newspapers, and Mrs Boehrer had talked about it in foreboding tones over lunch. Adolf Hitler, the monster himself, was coming to Dusseldorf this very day.

It was the first time he'd visited this part of Germany since coming to power. The city was holding a huge festival of so-called 'Aryan' German industry and culture. 'Aryan', in Nazi ideas, was supposed to mean 'pure German'. In other words, white, German-speaking and with German ancestry, but not Jewish or any of the other ethnic minorities despised by the Nazis. The exhibition was meant to show how wonderful the new Germany would be, with new designs for housing and public buildings, all built in the festival park. There were also displays of Nazi-approved art and science. No Jewish artists or scientists were included.

The Führer was coming in person to see the festival and give it his blessing, and the local Nazis were beside themselves with excitement and pride. Local schoolchildren – not only in Dusseldorf but in surrounding towns and villages – had been given a holiday. Most shops and businesses were closed for the day. So many people were pouring into the city for the big event that special buses had been arranged to transport them. That morning, on the way to work, the Rosenthal sisters had seen workers draping every building in the city centre with those hideous red, white and black swastika flags, supervised by Brownshirt storm troopers. The Hitler Youth boys and the League of German Girls were getting ready to parade and cheer for their beloved leader.

As Martha, Friedel and Gina walked on through the central streets, the crowds became a teeming throng; adults chattering excitedly, children clutching little swastika flags. It was nerve-racking for three Jewish girls, but there was no way to avoid it. They remembered the Nazi activities during the elections that had brought Hitler to power four years earlier. They recalled Mr Junkermann getting beaten up for not giving the Nazi salute. Back then, the Nazis had been a terrifying force, but at least they'd been a minority in Dusseldorf. Now it felt as if the whole city was out on the streets supporting them.

In King's Avenue, a broad, straight street with rows of trees on either side, people were lining the edge of the kerb. As the Rosenthal girls wove their way along as best they could, trying to look like ordinary Aryan citizens, the crowd suddenly began to erupt in deafening cheers. Children waved their flags wildly. People were chanting 'Germany! Germany!' and 'One people! One empire! One leader!' Above the shouting came the rhythmic crashing sound of soldiers marching.

'Let's have a look,' said Martha, and began sneaking in at the back of the crowd.

Friedel and Gina followed her reluctantly. They had vivid memories of what had happened to poor, proud Mr Junkermann, and just wanted to run for home.

Standing on tiptoe to see past people's heads and hats, they could just make out the steel helmets and slanted rifles of the marching soldiers. On and on they went, column after column. Then came the army motorcycles

and several big, gleaming Mercedes limousines driving slowly in procession. And then they saw *him*.

Hitler was standing in the front of his open-top limousine, dressed in his usual brown military uniform and peaked cap, his arm raised in the Nazi salute. The thin mouth beneath his little black moustache was twisted in a grin of triumph.

The sight chilled the Rosenthal sisters to their very bones. Martha murmured in Friedel's ear, 'A proper *Schweinehund* he looks, doesn't he?'

Friedel had to agree. The word means 'pig-dog'; in those days Germans used it to mean a horrible person.* Hitler really did look every bit the perfect *Schweinehund*.

Yet the people of Dusseldorf – or most of them, it seemed – adored him. Even worshipped him. It was as if a wave of madness had them in its grip, and they revelled in it. So many of them believed that this man, with his silly toothbrush moustache and bulging, manic eyes, was Germany's saviour. They were sure he would fix all their problems and make Germany strong again, and all Germans proud and contented. There were many tasks ahead. First of all, they had to get rid of all their left-wing political opponents. Then they would start building up Germany's industry and military forces. For all of this to

---

* The word *Schweinehund* is old-fashioned, and most Germans don't use it that way now. As a swear word, it used to be like calling someone a 'swine', a strong insult that is also very old-fashioned now.

work, the Nazis believed they would need to remove all the Jews.

The sisters walked the rest of the way home under a cloud of gloom and fear. What hope did they have, with so many people against them? So many seemingly ordinary folk now loathed them for no good reason. These people didn't even consider Jews to be real human beings.

It was difficult to believe that life could be any worse than this. And it was impossible to imagine that they were still only at the beginning of what the Nazis were capable of doing.

CHAPTER FOUR

The Secret of the Crossings

1938

The world had changed forever, and a life of freedom and joy existed only in memories and dreams. In the still of their coal office bedroom, the night sounds of the city were muffled by coal dust and sleep. Here, in dreams, the Rosenthal girls could escape the chilly city of *Now* into the sunny realm of *Before*.

Martha might dream of riding in the sidecar of Father's motorcycle on their way to another doctor's appointment. Or perhaps to the railway station, where she would set off on her annual summer holiday to the special hospital near Frankfurt. Martha loved it there. The air was clean and fresh, with green hills and forests. She adored the friends she'd made at the hospital and could still hear the happy chatter of the girls along the dining tables draped in crisp white tablecloths and decked with flowers. Martha grew stronger there, the joints of her arms and legs troubled her less.

Gina might dream of sweets in a paper cone, her fingers and lips sticky with sugar. And of running in the street with Bernard and the other boys of the neighbourhood. She might dream of that day when they went climbing on the building site, hand over hand, up the teetering scaffolding. Bernard dropped a brick and it hit Gina square on the head. The world tilted and jarred, and blood trickled down her face. It left her with a dent in her head ever after, but it did little to bruise her spirit of adventure. Or perhaps she dreamed of perfecting her harmonica playing, wreathed in gorgeous melodies.

In Friedel's dreams, she was on her bike, pedalling hard, swishing along a winding lane in the ancient sprawling woods of the Grafenberger Forest. It was so easy and so delicious to slip out from the smoke and racket of the city into pretty lanes. There you were shaded by birch, oak and beech trees, in grassy glades where deer grazed. The whole family, laden with sandwiches and flasks, would dine on the grass under the sun-dappled trees. Friedel and Gina and Bernard pedalled along behind Father, who sat upright and dignified even in his summer shirt and trouser clips. Martha followed along – she could ride a bike thanks to Father's devoted therapy sessions, but even though she was older she didn't have the strength of her brothers and sisters.

From time to time, Father would spot a spread of wild fruit growing beside the lane and raise his hand – 'Halt!' There was a squealing of brakes as they all pulled up to help him gather a crop of berries. They might be elderberries or wild gooseberries – purple and sour – or pungent blackberries, or sweet forest strawberries, bright scarlet among the scatter of white flowers. Friedel plucked them from their stems and felt their deliciousness unfold in her mouth.

Suddenly the dream turned dark and unpleasant. An ache was growing in her stomach. Not the stuffed discomfort from gorging on sandwiches and wild berries, but an ache of longing for this world that was gone forever...

Friedel woke, sweating and hugging her middle. The hard, thudding pain from the dream was still in her stomach. It gripped her insides like no pain she had ever known before, and she curled up, moaning.

Something was badly wrong. She needed help. The room around her was strange in the half-light from the window. She could hear Gina and Martha breathing, deep in sleep.

'Gina,' she whispered through her teeth, but the shape beside her in the bed didn't stir. '*Gina!*'

Her sister woke, rubbing her eyes. 'Wha's it?' she slurred sleepily.

'My tummy hurts,' Friedel gasped. 'Really, really bad. Go and fetch Mum.'

Gina looked doubtful at the thought of going into their parents' room, and perhaps waking Father by accident. 'Can't you go yourself?'

'I can't get up. It hurts too much.'

Martha was awake now. 'What are you two doing?' she said. 'I'm trying to sleep!'

'Friedel's tummy is bad.'

Martha got out of bed, lit a candle and came across the room. Martha was a proper grown-up now, just turned nineteen. Taking one look at Friedel's face, twisted in pain in the eerie candlelight, she hurried out of the room and tapped on their parents' bedroom door.

'Mum, Father, come quickly! Friedel's ill!'

Friedel was in so much pain the room around her was going in and out of focus. Time itself seemed to be elastic. Yellow candlelight swam around the walls, slowly giving way to grey daylight. Friedel was aware of worried faces – Mum, Father, Martha, Bernard, Gina – coming and going. She heard murmuring voices. The name *Dr Goldfarb* was mentioned several times.* It must be

---

* The name of the doctor is not recorded, so for simplicity I have given him this name.

serious – they had so little money these days, her parents must be truly worried if they were willing to spend some of it on a doctor. The Nazis had made it harder than ever for Jews to run businesses, and Father had been forced to give up his last one. They lived now mainly on their savings.

The whole of Friedel's world was centred on her belly and on the little patch of peeling, discoloured wallpaper beside her bed. She lay on her side, focusing on the wall, trying to pull her mind away from the pain.

She heard a man's voice. Mum's hand touched her shoulder. 'Let the doctor see you, Friedel,' she said.

Friedel looked up to see the face of Dr Goldfarb. He was a familiar sight to people in the neighbourhood around Germania Street; one of the handful of Jewish doctors who were still allowed to work.

Dr Goldfarb examined her belly, talking cheerily but looking deeply serious. When he'd finished, he led Mum and Father to the far corner of the room. They talked in low voices, but Friedel could make out some of what the doctor was saying.

'*Appendicitis ... borderline ... absolutely sure ... operation ... beyond me I'm afraid ... needs a hospital ...*'

At that last word, Mum went pale and Father glanced at Friedel, looking more grave than she'd ever seen him before. She could guess why. Jews had no rights any more, and were forbidden from all kinds of places – including most hospitals.

Mum and Father went out of the room with Dr Goldfarb. Martha came back in and sat down on the edge of the bed.

'Dr Goldfarb says it's your appendix. You know what that means?'

Friedel nodded unhappily. 'Will they do an operation on me?'

'Yes. They'll have to take it out. It's the only way to make you better.'

'Can the doctor do it?'

Martha shook her head. 'You need a hospital,' she said. 'Mum thinks she can get you into St Martinus – you know, the Catholic hospital.'

Friedel knew of it. After her experiences at school, the thought of going to another Catholic place would have made her quail – if she hadn't already been in such agony.

Of course, it wasn't so easy. Friedel couldn't simply go to hospital, because Jews weren't allowed any more. They had to make do with whatever medical care their local Jewish communities could provide. And with the Nazis restricting money and supplies, the communities could do little, so St Martinus was the only option. *If* Mum could get her in.

There was no time to lose. Friedel waited, curled up, fidgeting, staring at that patch of peeling wallpaper.

She knew how serious appendicitis could be. If it wasn't treated in time, you could die from it.

Father checked on her from time to time and Martha and Gina took turns trying to comfort her. They didn't have jobs to go to any more. Even Mrs Boehrer had lost her business. A change in the law had finally forced her to give up her shop and all her hard-won clients. A new, non-Jewish owner had taken it over, and they didn't employ Jewish workers.

At last, Mum came in looking triumphant. Friedel stared up blearily. 'They'll take you,' said Mum, smiling. 'You're going to be all right, my darling.'

Gina and Martha clapped their hands and exclaimed in delight.

'Be quiet and listen,' Father said. 'This is extremely important. Your mother has told the hospital that we are Catholic. You must *not* let the people there know you are a Jew. Do you understand? You must pretend to be a Catholic.'

Friedel shook her head. 'What? How?'

'On no account tell anyone you are Jewish. Do not mention that you know anyone Jewish. Do not reveal that you know any Jewish things. You know nothing of Shabbos. For you, Friedel, there is no Passover, nor any other Jewish holiday. Rosh Hashanah and Yom Kippur will be here soon, but you know nothing of them, my daughter, for you are Catholic, through and through.'

Rosh Hashanah is the traditional Jewish New Year, and Yom Kippur is the Day of Atonement. It is said that, for Jews on Rosh Hashanah, God decides your fate for the coming year, and on Yom Kippur it is written down and sealed in the great Book of Life. You must behave well every day between Rosh Hashanah and Yom Kippur to please God, so that your fate will be good. The Rosenthal family were not at all strict in their religion, but they went to synagogue for the main holy days, and Yom Kippur is the holiest of them all.

'None of that means anything to you,' said Mum. 'You don't know about those holidays. All you know is Catholic stuff – Christ and the Virgin Mary and Merry Christmas and Happy Easter.'

'Do you understand?' said Father. Friedel nodded. 'You know by now how important it is that they do not discover the truth.'

Friedel was in so much pain that she would agree to just about anything.

She knew some Catholic things from school: Mary and Joseph and Jesus on the cross. And of course nobody could avoid Christmas in Germany. Sometimes the important Jewish holiday of Hanukkah happened at the same time, but the Rosenthals always put up a Christmas tree, joining in with the general festivities.

'Remember to do the crossings,' said Gina.

Friedel was puzzled. 'The crossings? What are the crossings?'

'You know, how the teacher did at school. And there are prayers you have to say.'

Friedel didn't know the prayers, and she had no idea how to do these secret crossings, whatever they were.

While Mum and Gina helped Friedel out of bed and into a warm coat, fear began to grow in her. Before she knew it, their boots were clanging down the iron steps of the coal yard, then through the passage and out into Germania Street. It was only a kilometre to the hospital, but with her whole middle feeling as if she'd been kicked by a horse, Friedel could only go slowly, stooping like an elderly woman, with Mum helping her along. Even the short walk felt like a great trek.

At last they arrived in front of the hospital. St Martinus was a modern brick building with rows of little square windows, more like an office block than a hospital. Friedel and Mum looked with trepidation at the entrance, busy with people going in and out. They'd grown used to not being allowed inside buildings like this. But they plucked up their courage and went in through the doors.

Inside, it was like a cross between a hospital and a church. There was a strong smell of cleaning chemicals. People on crutches hobbled by. A child in a wheelchair rolled across the foyer. A few people were sitting and waiting, while doctors in white coats bustled about.

Instead of regular nurses, there were nuns, dressed in long black gowns that reached to the ground. On their heads they wore black headdresses with white bands round the forehead and neck, so that all you could see of them were their faces and hands. Each nun wore a heavy chain at her waist, from which hung a Christian cross.

Anxiously, Friedel huddled closer to Mum.

At last, one of the nuns noticed them and came gliding over, like a floating face in a pillar of black. The face had rosy cheeks and a warm, welcoming smile.

'Is this Friedel?' she said. Her voice was kind. 'Of course it is. We were told you were on your way.'

She clicked her fingers and, as if by magic, a man in a uniform appeared beside her with a wheelchair. Friedel was helped into it and was instantly wheeled away from her mother. The nun swished along ahead of her. There was a corridor, then a clanking lift, then another corridor, and finally Friedel found herself in a bright room.

There were four iron-framed beds with fat white pillows and a table covered with a floral cloth in the middle of the room. A washstand with a white metal basin stood beside the window. On the wall was a cross with the figure of Jesus nailed to it, like the ones they'd had in school. There were two other girls in the room. They looked curiously at Friedel as she was wheeled in and helped into bed.

A doctor came in and asked her questions about her pain. Unlike the friendly nuns, the doctor was rather cold-eyed and didn't smile. He examined her and agreed that her appendix was the problem.

'It has to come out,' he said. 'Most urgently. You should have come in sooner,' he added crossly, as if the delay was Friedel's fault.

With that, he left the room, followed by the nun. The door closed. Friedel was left to herself, her only company the two strange girls and Jesus on the cross.

Evening was drawing in, and it was soon time for the patients to go to bed. The two other girls knelt beside their beds and began their nightly prayer. Friedel copied

them, getting down on her knees in spite of the pain and putting her hands together.

She mumbled along with the prayer, following the words as she heard them – 'My God and Father, I thank thee for all thy graces during this day. I am sorry for all the sins I have committed and promise with thy help not to sin again. Holy Father, bless my family and have mercy on those souls in Purgatory.'

Friedel stumbled over the unfamiliar word 'Purgatory'. It is the place where Catholics believe they go after they die, before they're allowed into Heaven. Purgatory is said to be a miserable place, where people are made better through suffering before gaining the right to enter Heaven. Catholics offer prayers to help the poor souls in Purgatory on their way.

When the prayer was finished, the girls said 'Amen' and made the sign of the cross on themselves, touching their forehead then their tummy, then the left and right of their chest. So *that* was what Gina had been talking about! Friedel watched from the corner of her eye and imitated them.

It was almost impossible to sleep in the unfamiliar room. It smelled of antiseptic, and strange hospital noises leaked through the door – the chatter of voices, trolley wheels trundling, distant doors slamming. Friedel listened to the other girls breathing, and it was almost as if she were in her own room with Martha and Gina.

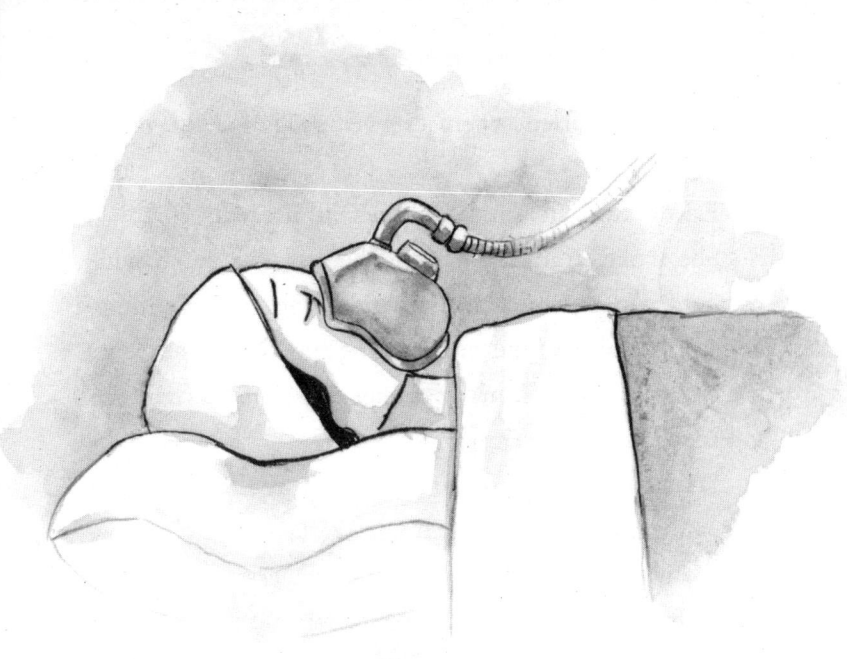

Friedel must have drifted into sleep, because she was suddenly wakened by the light coming on and nuns swooping round her bed like giant crows. Before she knew what was happening, she was bundled on to a hospital trolley and wheeled out of the room.

A corridor ceiling whizzed by overhead, with flashes of light. There was a lift again, then yet another corridor, then she was in a bright room with white tiles on the wall and shining metal cabinets. Doctors peered down at her, and a big metal mask was lowered over her mouth and nose. One of the doctors dripped a liquid into the top of the mask. There was a sharp, powerful chemical smell. Almost instantly the room swam and swirled, then everything faded to black silence.

Friedel was back in the universe of dreams.

She woke, confused, to find herself in a room with daylight coming through the window. It seemed strange at first, but slowly the pieces came together – the beds, the cross on the wall, and the other two girls sitting at the table, reading and writing.

Friedel's belly still hurt badly. But it was different, more of a burning pain, and it didn't make her feel sick like it had before. Probing gently with her fingers, she found a thick dressing covering the area where they'd done the operation.

It had been a success! Not just the operation but the whole plan. She'd fooled them into thinking she was a Catholic. They had fixed her. She'd be all right now.

Friedel heard a man's voice in the corridor outside, and shoe heels clacking on the hard floor. The voice sounded annoyed about something. The door burst open, making Friedel and the other two girls jump, and the doctor came into the room, followed by two nuns. His eyes had been cold before, but now they blazed with anger.

He glared at Friedel, then barked at the nuns, 'How has this been allowed to occur? Who is responsible?'

The nuns mumbled, apologising, casting anxious glances towards Friedel. 'She's a child, sir, she needs our care. It's surely right and Christian to –'

'She's a Jew!' the doctor snapped. 'A Jew, in *my* hospital!'

Friedel stared in alarm and bewilderment. She couldn't even begin to guess how they'd found out. The pain in her middle gave way to a cold knot of fear.

The doctor barked, 'Get her out of here! Out, out! This instant!'

'We can't cast her out, sir!' said one of the nuns. 'The poor child's just had surgery.'

'Then put her in a separate room at least. Hide her. And get rid of her as soon as you can. If the authorities find out we've treated one of them here . . .'

Leaving the words hanging in the air, he gave one last furious look at Friedel, then strode out.

The nuns helped Friedel get out of bed. If anything they were even kinder than they had been before, as if ashamed of the doctor.

Followed by the hostile stares of the two girls – whose names she would never know – Friedel was wheeled out and taken to another room. There were no other patients here. Despite the kindness of the nuns, who made sure she had anything she needed, Friedel felt dirty and filled with shame.

She stayed for a couple of days in the room. By then, she'd recovered enough to be taken home. It was good to be back with Mum and Father and her sisters and brother. The wound in her tummy would heal, but the wound in her heart never would. A lot had happened since Hitler came to power, but it was only now that Friedel truly understood just how bad things were.

Every day the Nazis made the Jews suffer in ways nobody could have imagined before, along with all the other people they hated. It was starting to seem as if there were no limits to what they might do in the future.

CHAPTER FIVE

A Bag of Beans

Autumn came, but these days it was as if all times of the year were the same. There was no work to go to for the Rosenthal family, little money, and no outings or other pleasures to spend it on. All they could do was exist from day to day as the weather grew colder.

In late October, the greatest shock of all fell on the little household in the dusty coal offices. In the depths of a chilly night, a thunderous banging on the front door echoed along the corridor.

It pounded its way into the sleeping heads of the three girls, whose bedroom was closest to the door. All three of them sat bolt upright in bed, gasping, staring into the darkness.

BANG! BANG! BANG!

A man's voice called out, 'Open up!'

Martha lit a candle, turning the darkness into a thick yellow gloom. In its flickering light the three sisters' faces were ghostly and wide-eyed.

Padding along the corridor to their parents' room, Martha tapped with her knuckles and opened it. 'Father,' she hissed. 'Somebody's knocking at the door.'

It came again – *BANG! BANG! BANG!* – and the voice shouted, 'Open this door! This is the police. We know you're in there.'

Father came out in his dressing gown, with Mum following after, both bleary and startled. Friedel and Gina peeped warily out of their door. Bernard came out of his room, looking terrified.

Going to the front door, Father straightened himself, mustering as much dignity as he could in pyjamas and slippers, and opened it.

A dazzling glare of torchlight blasted the family's eyes. 'Abraham Rosenthal?' said the voice.

'That is correct,' said Father. 'What is the matter?'

The torchlight shifted, and Friedel made out the distinctive shiny-buttoned uniforms of two policemen standing in the doorway. Nowadays, a police uniform meant just one thing: *Nazi*. And if you were a Jew, it meant one other thing: *Be afraid*.

One of the policemen held out a piece of paper to Father, and said gruffly, 'This is an expulsion order. I'm going to need everyone's passports.'

Stunned, Father took the paper. It was a printed form, with official stamps on it. 'What does this mean?'

'It means you get out now, Jew. Out of this house, out of Germany. You're coming with us.'

'But it's the middle of the night. We're not dressed. The children –'

The policeman ignored him. 'Take what you can carry, nothing more. And be quick.' He clapped his hands. 'Quickly now! Quickly!'

It was as if the whole family had been electrocuted. They were stunned by horror and confusion. The children all looked at Mum and Father.

'Passports,' said the policeman. '*Now.*'

Father hurried off and came back a moment later with the family's passports – his, Mum's and Martha's. The policeman took them, flicked through the pages and pocketed them.

Meanwhile, Mum pulled herself together and started organising Martha and the kids. 'Get dressed. Be quick, like the man says. One bag each, essentials only. Pick warm clothes. Oh, and food – I expect we'll have to take food.'

Friedel and Gina followed Martha back into their room. The covers were thrown back from their beds where they'd jumped out of them. Had that really been only a few minutes ago? The body-warmth in the sheets was quickly fading into the chilly air. It was like the last faint trace of their cosy old life disappearing.

In this moment, with that knock on the door, everything had changed forever. All of us have woken up from a nightmare at some time; the Rosenthal children had woken *into* one.

The Rosenthals were even more unlucky than most other Jews. Not only were they Jewish, they were Polish as well – even Friedel, Gina, Bernard and Max, who were born in Germany, were seen as Polish, not German. That made them doubly unwelcome and unwanted.

That was bad enough, but it wasn't only the Nazis in Germany who disliked Jews. The Polish government was also hostile – although not in quite the same way. Mum and Father had been forced to leave there in 1920 because of violence against Jews in their town. Now the government in Poland announced that any Polish people living in other countries would no longer be Polish citizens. To avoid that, they had to travel back right away and fill in a lot of forms, which was impossible for most of them. Since nearly all the people affected by this were Jews, it seemed that the Polish government's intention was to get rid of a lot of Jewish people. The Nazis were horrified at the idea of being stuck with so many Jews, and decided to throw them out of Germany as quickly as they could.

With the policemen shouting insults at them and ordering them to hurry, Mum, Martha, Gina, Bernard and Friedel rushed about in confusion, in and out of rooms, pulling open cupboards and drawers, snatching up bags and throwing things into them. In a haze of panic, Friedel bundled stuff into a bag. Rushing to the kitchen, she glanced frantically around. What food to take? Spotting a big paper bag of dried beans, she grabbed it, without really thinking why. It was just there, so she took it. Back in the bedroom, she picked up a spare pair of shoes. No reason, they were just there. Maybe she'd need them, who could tell?

The policeman in charge went through Father's wallet. 'Your limit for cash you can take with you is ten marks,' he

said, leafing through the thin sheaf of banknotes. Marks – or Reichsmarks to give them their proper name – were the German currency in those days. Satisfied that Father had far less than ten marks,* the policeman handed the wallet back.

Martha carefully packed her favourite doll, Leni. Although Martha was a grown-up now, Leni was still very precious to her. She'd been made specially for Martha when she was fighting against her polio, and Father had given the doll to her as a reward after the first time she

---

* About £380 in today's money.

managed to walk. Leni's hair was real, made from Mum's beautiful blonde locks. All the sisters – Martha, Friedel and Gina – regarded Leni as if she were their mother in miniature. It would be unthinkable to leave her behind.

Soon everyone was ready to leave – or as ready as they could be in the little time they were given. The policemen shepherded them harshly out of the front door. In the still night air, the sound of their heels on the metal stairs was more dismal than ever.

A police van was waiting in the street. Father asked where they were being taken. One of the policemen said, 'You're going to the Ulm.' Father's face went pale. 'The Ulm' was the nickname of the city's prison. It had gained a terrifying reputation since the Nazis took over. It was where they locked up people who opposed them.

The sisters huddled together in the back of the van as it roared through the streets. Mum held them close, along with Bernard. Father sat opposite, looking white as a sheet. Bernard was forcing himself not to show fear even though he felt like crying. Friedel felt numb and tingling. She hugged the paper bag of beans the way someone drowning would cling to a life jacket. The bag crackled and strained.

After about twenty minutes, the van halted and the rear doors swung open. Torches glared, and the Rosenthals were bundled out into a cobbled yard. Looming above them in the lamplight was a stone building, forbidding and ugly – the prison's front wing. Father and Bernard were taken away separately, to be put in the men's wing. Mum and the girls were herded through a series of huge clanging iron gates and eventually found themselves inside one of the main cell blocks in the women's wing.

Very long and two storeys high, the women's wing was like a vast hall. On each of the upper levels, landings with steel rails lined both sides, looking over the central area. The landings were all connected by metal staircases. Along each level were dozens of iron cell doors.

A prison guard led them up one of the staircases. The sound of boots on metal seemed like a horrible music they were doomed to listen to forever. Friedel hugged the beans even tighter, and as she did so, the paper finally gave way. The bag split, sending a swooshing cascade of dry beans down the stairs, hundreds upon hundreds of them tinkling and bouncing through the gaps, showering down through the air like a hailstorm.

Friedel stood with the torn bag, shaking with grief and fear, as the last few beans trickled out of it. Mum took her by the arm and gently led her the rest of the way up the stairs.

Mum and the three girls were put in a cell together. It had two bunk beds for the four of them to share and a chamber pot for a toilet. The heavy iron door clanged loudly behind them and the key snicked in the lock.

Their heads teemed with questions. What was going

to happen to them? If they were being sent to Poland, why were they in prison? Where were Bernard and Father?

Of course the guards couldn't or wouldn't tell them anything, so the questions kept on going round and round. Mum and the three girls lay on their bunks and tried to sleep. The prison echoed with the clanking of doors and the footsteps of guards on the landings. From time to time there were shouts and cries, and someone somewhere screamed, perhaps in a nightmare, perhaps from something worse.

* * *

The next day, the Rosenthals were let out of the cell to wash, empty the chamber pot, and be fed. They discovered that they were not the only family in their situation. Far from it. All along their landing, the cells contained other Jewish-Polish women and girls. They were all as confused and upset as the Rosenthals, and worrying about what had been done with their husbands, sons and brothers.

All over Dusseldorf, Polish Jews were being arrested and brought to the prison. As the day wore on, the place quickly became overcrowded. The Rosenthals found themselves sharing their cell with three other women, all strangers. Nobody knew what was going on.

Breakfast was the same stuff the regular prisoners ate – bread and porridge. The bread was the dark brown, heavy kind that Germans call *Schwarzbrot*: 'black bread'. The Rosenthal children hated its sour, nasty taste. The porridge was half-congealed and stiff as mashed potato. As hungry as they were, they couldn't eat much of it.

The day went by with no answers, then another day, and then another. Soon it was as if this teeming prison hall with its grim iron doors was to be their new home.

On the third day, the guards and police came and announced that it was time to go. The cell doors swung open, and the bewildered people were herded along the landing and down the stairs, back through the series of great gates, and out into the cold evening air.

With their handfuls of belongings, they were put on special buses, with police guarding them closely to make sure nobody ran off. After a short drive, they reached the central railway station. All the Rosenthals knew this place well. One of Father's shops had been near here. For Martha, the station was the happy place where she had set off each summer for her special holidays to help her polio. But now, instead of going through the main hall, the women and children were marched to the area where goods trains passed through. There was no platform, just the tracks and the loose stones.

They were joined by another stream of prisoners – the men and boys. There were cries of relief and joy as the women and girls found their husbands, sons and fathers among the swirling crowd. Looking a bit more tired

and unkempt than the last time they'd seen him, Father appeared, with Bernard beside him.

A train was waiting on the tracks. There were no passenger coaches, just a long line of goods wagons, made of wood, like boxes on wheels, with no windows and no seats inside. The people were forced into the dark, dank, smelly wagons, and the big doors slid shut.

Inside the Rosenthals' wagon it was pitch black, with nothing but the sounds and smells of dozens of people packed tightly together. There was whispered, anxious chatter. Some people prayed softly. A few of the younger children were crying, and their mothers were trying to comfort them. From outside, they heard shouts – nasty, angry, and filled with insults against the Jews. Footsteps crunched back and forth on the stones. One by one, the wagon doors closed in a series of grinding crashes.

There was a jolt, a clang of couplings, and slowly the train began to move.

Mum and Father must have imagined going back home to Poland many times, but they could never have guessed it would be like this. As for the children, Germany was the only home they had ever known. Martha had been born in Poland, but they'd left when she was still a baby.

Even so, there was one glimmer of hope. Hans was in Poland. According to his letters, he was doing all right, so maybe the rest of the family would be fine too. At this moment, hope was what they needed, more than anything.

CHAPTER SIX

Zbaszyn

It was a long journey. Dusseldorf is near the far western edge of Germany, Poland is to the east, and Germany is a big country. It was a trip of over seven hundred kilometres, and took all night.

The train journey was truly horrible, with dozens of people packed inside the closed wagon. Nothing to sit on, no toilets. The only light was a few glimmers of daylight through gaps in the wooden walls.

At last, the train slowed and came to a halt. The door of the wagon rumbled open. Although it was a gloomy winter day, it dazzled the people inside after they'd spent hours in darkness. Friedel and Gina, Martha and Bernard, Mum and Father all heaved themselves up from the floor and staggered out.

They found themselves on a station platform. A sign painted in big black capital letters gave the name of the place:

ZBASZYN*

From the spelling it was clearly a Polish name, but Friedel and Gina had never heard of it. Very few people had. Zbaszyn was a tiny town huddled up against the border between Poland and Germany, and being on the border was the only thing that made it at all important. It was here that most of the Polish Jews from Germany were being dropped off. The German government had transported them this far, and now it was Poland's responsibility to deal with them. Unfortunately, the Polish government had no intention of dealing with them. If Poland had wanted these people, they would never have ended up in this situation in the first place.

Making sure they had their few belongings, hundreds of people slowly filed off the platform into the station building. The Rosenthals had no idea where to go or what to do, so they went into the ticket hall and found places to settle down and rest. It was crowded and there

---

* Polish words can be tricky for English speakers to say. Zbaszyn is pronounced *Z'bon-shin* (even though it doesn't have an *n* in the middle, you say one). Many German speakers say it as *Sponsheen*. Friedel and Gina said it like that.

were hardly any benches. Gina hauled herself up on to the ticket counter and sat with her back resting on the pillar. The rest of the family sat down on the floor.

Father went and asked around to see if anybody knew anything about what would happen next. Everyone was asking the same question. *Would they be able to travel onwards from here, to the places they knew, to the towns they had lived in in the old days?* Nobody knew the answer. Mum and Father came originally from a city called Czestochowa,* but that was a long way from here, down in the south of Poland.

Up on the counter, Gina was beginning to doze. She was exhausted, and it was lovely and warm in the station after such a long, cold journey. Even on this uncomfortable perch she felt herself drifting off. As the darkness of sleep closed round her, her bottom began to slip on the polished wood. She jerked awake, but too late – arms flailing, with a yelp she fell with a crash on Mum's legs.

'Oooowww!' Mum wailed. 'Gina, you foolish girl! My ankle, I think you've broken it!' She touched it gingerly, wincing. 'That's all we need, me with a broken leg.'

While this was going on, Martha noticed that some kids – local Polish kids by the look of them – were weaving through the crowds. They had a shifty look about them. Suddenly one of them made a grab for someone's suitcase.

---

* This name is also pronounced with an invisible *n*: *Chen-sto-hova*.

There were yells of outrage from the people nearby as he ran with it out of the station. Over the next hour, the same thing kept on happening. Taking advantage of the people's exhaustion and bewilderment, the Polish kids managed to steal a lot of bags and suitcases.

The people they stole from were devastated. They had few belongings, and the less you have, the more precious it becomes. Most of them, in the panic of being arrested, had packed their most treasured possessions, their little stock of money and their valuable bits of jewellery, which might have been used to buy food or shelter. All gone now. Martha and the other Rosenthals kept a sharp eye out, and fortunately nothing of theirs was taken.

Father had gone out exploring the area near the station, trying to find somewhere for them to stay. After an hour or two he returned.

'I've found a stable,' he said.

Mum stared at him. 'A what?'

'There's a stable nearby. It looks dry and comfortable – as much as a stable can.'

'A *stable*?' said Mum, aghast. 'Do we look like horses?'

Father's lips tightened. 'It is the best I can provide, Helene. More suitable than here, I promise. We should hurry before others find it.'

He was right. It was warm in the station, but the floor was hard and it was so crowded that many people out on the platform couldn't even get in.

Mum had to be helped to her feet, wincing and gasping. Her leg wasn't broken, but she could hardly put her weight on it. Supporting her, they left the station and followed Father down the street, gazing around curiously at their surroundings.

Zbaszyn was a strange sight to kids who'd grown up in a city. It seemed half like a town, with some big buildings, but also half like the countryside, with farms and fields in among them.

After a short walk along a dirt lane, they came to the stable. It was a large building, which belonged to a Polish cavalry regiment. Venturing inside, they were met by

the powerful smell of hay and horses. The big animals shifted and huffed in their stalls as the Rosenthals looked around for a place to settle down. Father found a dry corner where straw had been strewn thickly over the cobblestones. Friedel and Gina sat on it, shivering, while Father and Martha tried to make Mum comfortable. Bernard sat staring at nothing, lost in his own thoughts.

For a while the Rosenthals were alone with the horses. But as Father had predicted, others soon discovered the stable. Before long the place was full of cold, hungry people. They milled about, trying in vain to find somewhere to lie down, or squatted, hunched up in their overcoats and hats, hugging their bags and cases. It was a miserable, uncomfortable night. Exhausted as they were, sleep was all but impossible.

The next morning, Father went out exploring again. After a few hours he returned. He'd found them somewhere a bit better than a stable – a hayloft in a barn. So once more they followed him along the muddy lanes to a street on the edge of the town, right beside the railway line.

'I made an agreement with the lady who owns it,' Father said, leading them across the street and between the houses to a small barn. It was filled with hay, some in bales, some piled loose. There was a ladder to the upper floor, where the hayloft was.

Mum stared at it. 'An agreement? You mean we're paying for this?'

Father didn't look as if he wanted a discussion. 'Up there,' he said, pointing to the hayloft. 'It should be dry and comfortable enough at least.'

The kids swarmed up the ladder and found a dingy, musty-smelling loft heaped with hay. It was comfortable to lie on – just like a downy mattress, if you ignored the smell and the scratchiness.

They heard Mum's voice from below. 'I can't do it, Abraham. My leg.' Looking down, Friedel and Gina saw Mum trying to climb the ladder. With her bad leg it was simply impossible. She gave up and sat on a hay bale. 'You go on up. I'll stay down here.'

Father wasn't having that. He walked across to the owner's house, went up the steps and knocked on the door. A woman opened it.

They couldn't hear what was being said, but the woman looked across at the barn, frowned and shook her head. Father brought out his wallet and offered some of his precious little stock of cash. The woman hesitated, then nodded and took the money.

'We are saved,' said Father, returning to the barn. 'Mrs Nowak will let us have a room in the house.'

Again they followed him. Mrs Nowak led them up the stairs to a room at the end of the landing. It was almost completely bare. A garden bench and a few hard chairs were the only furniture.

As they started to settle in, Friedel went and looked

out of the window at the street. Its name was Wigury Street. It was narrow, lined with large houses all spaced out. This house – number 9 – was near the end, where the road petered out into wasteland, with a tangle of brambles and trees next to the railway line. Friedel was half-expecting to be leaving here at any moment, to go trekking again in search of something better. She didn't know it then, but this room was to be their home for a while to come.

As with the stable, it didn't take long for others to discover 9 Wigury Street. Almost every house and building in Zbaszyn was being sought out by the desperate Jews from Germany. It wasn't only the hundreds who'd come from Dusseldorf; thousands more were arriving from places all over Germany, and the little town was soon completely overwhelmed. There were more than six thousand new arrivals altogether, which was more than the number of people who already lived in the town. Most arrived by train like the Rosenthals, but others had been dropped on the German side of the border and were forced to walk across at gunpoint.

Even if the Polish townsfolk wanted to help the poor refugees – and many of them did help, especially the local Jewish people – there wasn't much they could do for so many.

The arrival of the refugees alarmed the Polish government. They didn't want *any* of these people to come, let alone the thousands being unloaded from the trains. The government panicked, fearing that the refugees would spread out across Poland. And so, the same day the Rosenthals arrived, the government banned anyone from Germany from leaving Zbaszyn. People like the Rosenthals, who'd been hoping to travel on to where their relations lived, were bitterly disappointed.

Right away, the bare upstairs room at 9 Wigury Street began to fill up. The Rosenthals themselves were six people – Mum, Father, Friedel, Gina, Martha and Bernard. By the end of the first day, they were joined by a man and his two teenage sons. Then another man who had no family came and found a corner to settle in. So that made ten people, all living in one room. The second upstairs room also quickly filled up with people. Old people, kids, people alone, and whole families were wandering all over Zbaszyn in search of somewhere to shelter and lay their heads.

The families living at number 9 had no facilities to wash their clothes or clean their teeth. The only way to wash themselves was a tap outside. They scrubbed their faces and hands with cold water in the icy air and had to be content with it.

After a few days, help came from the Red Cross, an international charity that assists refugees and people affected by wars, famines and other catastrophes. The Rosenthals and their roommates were given sack-like

mattresses to sleep on, as well as toothbrushes and toothpaste. The mattresses filled up the floor space at night and were rolled up and stacked in the daytime. A table was found to sit at and eat from.

Best of all, the Red Cross set up outdoor kitchens in the town, which served hot food to the refugees. Each day, Father would go to the nearest kitchen with either Friedel or Gina, carrying bowls and a big metal canister in which to bring back their dinner. There were always crowds and a long queue. The Red Cross workers doled out a thin, watery soup, and the Rosenthals would trudge back to Wigury Street, the soup quickly going cold as they walked.

As the days turned into weeks, it became clear that no help would be coming from the Polish government. For the Jewish refugees, Zbaszyn would turn out to be like the place called Purgatory that the kids had learned of in Catholic school – the place where souls suffered while hoping to be let into Heaven. Unfortunately, nothing heavenly was on offer for the poor people of Zbaszyn. The best they could pray for was that they wouldn't end up in Hell.

CHAPTER SEVEN

The Soldier

1939

'So,' said Mr Becker. 'Tell me how you would say the sentence, *My name is Friedel.*'

'My name is Friedel,' said Friedel in German.

Mr Becker shook his head. 'No, no, no, girl. I want to hear how you would say it *in English*, if you please.'

Friedel frowned, concentrating hard, and pronounced, 'Mine nem ist . . . iss Friedel.'

Mr Becker was a patient teacher, and he smiled encouragingly. 'That's better. But still rather imperfect. Try again.'

'May name iss Friedel.'

'Hmph. Now Martha, you try.'

Martha said carefully, 'Mine name iss Martha.'

'Not bad at all. Now you, Regina.'

'My name is Gina,' said Gina in English.

Mr Becker beamed. 'Wonderful. Just perfect.'

The Rosenthals had been in Zbaszyn for several weeks now, still living crammed into one room with the other refugees. Mr Becker lived in the room next door. He'd been a teacher before the Nazis sent him to Zbaszyn. He'd loved his job, and as soon as he got to know the Rosenthals he offered to help the three girls learn English.

Friedel found it a hard slog – she just couldn't get her tongue round the difficult English sounds. You learned to say a word, and then, when you saw a word with some of the same letters, they often turned out to be said in a completely different way. It was extremely confusing. Think of words like *through*, *though*, *cough* and *thought*. Or *book*, *roof* and *door*, and you can understand how hard it is. In German, letters mostly sound the same no matter which words they're in. Martha had a bit less trouble than Friedel did, but it was Gina who took to English most easily. The peculiar sounds seemed to give her no trouble at all. Gina was Mr Becker's star student.

But living the way they were, it was impossible for them to learn properly, and none of the girls had made much progress. It was frustrating for them, and for Mr Becker, who longed for his old life in the classroom.

When the lesson was over, the girls went back to their room. Friedel rested her arms on the window frame and gazed down at Wigury Street. It was a bitterly cold winter day. The bright sunshine cast long shadows along the dirty road, but did little to warm the air.

Mum came and stood beside her. 'What are you looking at, Friedel?'

'Oh, nothing. Just the street.'

She was staring out across the flat countryside beyond the railways lines when she suddenly sensed Mum's body going tense.

Mum gasped. 'Look! Look there!'

Friedel looked. Mum was pointing down the street. A lone Polish soldier was walking along the edge of the road. He wore a peaked cap and khaki-green army overcoat. Friedel peered at him, but couldn't understand why Mum was so excited.

'It's him! Abraham, children, it's him, he's here!'

Mum rushed from the window and hurried down the stairs as fast as she could, with Friedel and the rest of the family trailing after her. Out of the front door she went and down the steps.

In the street she halted, as if overcome, as the soldier walked towards her.

He was a handsome young man, as he always had been, even back in the days when he sold newspapers and cakes in the shop. Although Friedel hadn't seen him for three years, it took her only a moment to recognise her big brother.

'Hans!' cried Mum, throwing her arms round him. 'Oh Hans! My dear child!'

He hugged her, grinning. 'Not a child any more, Mum. Look at me!'

Mum reached up and held his face in her hands. Tears were flowing down her cheeks. 'However did you find us? How did you know?'

Hans's smile faded. 'I heard what they did to our people, those Nazis. I figured out you'd be in Zbaszyn, so I came and asked around.' He shrugged. 'It's quite a community you've got going here. Sooner or later you meet someone who knows someone who knows the people you're looking for.'

By now the rest of the family had caught up with Mum – Friedel, Martha, Gina, Bernard, Father. Everyone was weeping with joy. Nearly three years had passed since they'd last seen Hans. He seemed so different now, a proper grown-up man, and a soldier like he'd always dreamed of being. And yet he was still the big brother the girls and Bernard knew.

There was a lot of catching up to do. So much had happened to the family since Hans had last heard from them. He listened in growing dismay to the story of how they'd been treated. There was an additional worry, too. Max was no longer living in the farming community near Berlin. He'd avoided being sent to Zbaszyn, and was trying to get to England. If he managed it, he'd be safe for now, but Mum and Father were terribly worried about him.

Hans had news of his own. He was married now, with a baby on the way. His wife, a little bit confusingly, was called Martha. They had a home near the city of Warsaw, although Hans was on duty with the army nearly all the time.

Sitting at the table in the room the family shared, Hans told them news from the world outside Zbaszyn. One by one, the other inhabitants of the room drifted close, eager to hear what was going on. Including the Rosenthal family, there were seventeen women, men and children crammed into that one room.

The news was worrying. There was no sign of either the Polish or the German government doing anything to help the Zbaszyn refugees. And there was no likelihood of them being allowed to travel on into Poland. There was tension between Poland and Germany. Not just about this issue, but about many other disagreements. Many believed that Hitler wanted to take over Poland.

Earlier that year, Nazi Germany had conquered Austria. The official reason was that, since Austrians spoke German, they should be seen as Germans – so long as they were Aryan. Therefore Austria had to become part of Germany. Living in Poland were a great many people who had German ancestors and who spoke German, but were officially Polish. They were known as *Volksdeutsche*,* which means 'German people'. The Nazis – who despised Polish people almost as much as Jews – believed that the *Volksdeutsche* needed to be part of Germany too. And it seemed that one way to do that would be to invade Poland. Austria had become part of Germany willingly, without a war. Poland would not.

This was scary for the Rosenthals, not just because of the threat of Nazis coming to Poland. If a war happened, Hans would have to fight.

At last it was time for Hans to depart. He was on a short leave (time off from the army) at the moment, and had a long journey to Warsaw ahead of him. As he began to say his goodbyes, Mum couldn't bear it. She needed to at least have a memento of her son to hold on to. So once again the camera was brought out to capture this special family occasion.

Everyone in the room got involved. They had started to become almost like a huge family now, and Mum and Father sat at the head of the table for the photo, with the girls standing behind them and Hans and Bernard crowding close to Mum. All the other people and their kids sat round the table and beamed for the camera.

After that, everyone – the whole family and their roommates – trooped downstairs to say goodbye to Hans and pose for another photo on the front steps. It took a

---

* This is pronounced *Follks-doytsh*.

long time to get ready. The sun was bright, but it was a bitterly cold Polish winter day, and they all got wrapped up in their big overcoats, scarves and hats.

Hans stood at the front, and Mum hooked her arm through his, holding him tight. She was so proud of him, but also grieving at having to let him go.

After Hans had gone, a feeling of loss settled over the family. The news they'd learned from him was not hopeful for the future.

* * *

Winter dragged by for the lost souls of Zbaszyn. As the months passed, there was no sign of anything changing. Poland and Germany talked and disagreed and talked and disagreed some more.

With little hope of ever reaching their old home towns in Poland, some of the refugees started trying to leave Poland entirely. They began applying to emigrate to other countries.

America was the most popular choice. A lot of Jewish Americans had originally emigrated to America from Germany, Poland and Russia (or their parents or grandparents had). They often kept in touch with their cousins and other relatives left behind in the old countries. Now these American Jews became a lifeline.

Ever since the rise of the Nazis, thousands of emigration applications had been filled in by German Jews, and thousands of Jewish Americans had offered to help support their relatives if they came to America. But the Nazi government made it as difficult as possible, and so did the American government. There was a lot of negative feeling in America about immigrants and refugees, especially Jewish ones coming from Nazi Germany. So, the Americans kept a very tight limit on the number who were let in.

The Rosenthals were among the thousands who applied. It was a slender hope. Father had a cousin in the American city of Cleveland. He was a distant cousin, and difficult to get in touch with. A Jewish charity was trying to help the people in Zbaszyn get to America, and Father gave them his cousin's details. But as the weeks passed, nothing came of it.

Life went on in Zbaszyn. In a way, it thrived. The refugees from Germany built up their own community, with social clubs and youth groups. People got together to chat or play cards. Often proper entertainments were organised, like singing or putting on traditional Jewish plays based on old folk stories.

They carved out a life as best they could, trying to act as if all of this was normal. It was difficult, but they managed. For families like the Rosenthals, who at least had a proper roof over their heads, it wasn't too terrible. The majority, though, were living in awful accommodation, either in old army barracks or in the town's big disused flour mill. They were helped a little by Jewish charities in other countries, who collected money for aid.

And then, as summer was warming the lands around them, the people in Zbaszyn received joyful news: at long last they were allowed to leave. They'd all been hoping against hope that this day would come. Finally, the Rosenthals were free to travel on to Czestochowa, the place that Mum and Father had left nearly twenty years ago.

The arrangements were tricky. Both of them had relatives there, including Father's sisters, but none of them was particularly well off. Father's sisters were ready to do what they could, but it might not be very much. The family had hardly any money left, and would have nowhere to live, other than in the spare rooms of their relatives. It was the Rosenthals' first glimpse of freedom in nine months, though, and they were happy.

CHAPTER EIGHT

Going Home

Another school, another day of puzzlement and confusion. Once again Friedel and Gina found themselves sitting at a desk, on a hard wooden bench, gazing unhappily at an unfamiliar teacher. It was almost like their first day at the Catholic school, all those years ago. They were fifteen years old now, not six, but it was still scary and miserable.

Their new school was at least Jewish. That was the only good thing about it. Everyone spoke Polish all the time, which neither Friedel nor Gina understood. It wasn't really a proper school – just a classroom in a Jewish orphanage, a place where children who don't have families live. The twins weren't orphans, but it had begun to feel as if they were. The orphanage was in the city of Lodz,* over a hundred kilometres away from Czestochowa, where most of their family were now living.

When the family had been allowed to leave Zbaszyn, the hope had been that they'd all go to Czestochowa to join their relatives. But none of them had enough room for all the Rosenthal family – even without Max or Hans, there were still six of them. Father's sister, Aunt Henne, helped out, but she had six children of her own, and there was no room at all for Bernard or the twins. So the three of them had been sent to Lodz, where another of Father's sisters, Aunt Zura, lived. Instead of taking them in to live with her, Aunt Zura arranged places for them in the city. Bernard was now living in a Jewish centre where a lot of refugee boys from Germany were staying, while Friedel and Gina had been placed in this orphanage. They hated it. They were as unhappy as they had ever been in their lives.

'I miss Mum,' said Friedel one evening, staring down into her bowl of watery soup. She said the same thing pretty much every day, and if she didn't say it, she just quietly felt it – the pain of being outside the warm circle of Mum's love.

'Me too,' said Gina. 'I miss Father as well.'
'And Martha.'
'I miss Bernard,' said Gina miserably. 'I wish he was

---

* This is pronounced as *Wodge* or sometimes *Lodge*.

here. This place would be so much more fun with him.' She picked at her slice of bread; it was far from fresh. A thought came to her, and she glanced around to check nobody was listening. 'We should go,' she said.

'Go? What do you mean?'

'Run away! Escape!' Gina's eyes brightened. 'We could go to Czestochowa and find Mum and Father.'

Friedel's heart leapt at the idea. But then she quailed at the thought of how far away Czestochowa was. In between was a whole swathe of Poland, unknown to them and filled with people whose language they couldn't speak. 'How would we even get there?'

'By train, of course. We'll get money and just take off!' Gina smiled. 'We just need to figure out how to get the money.'

'We could ask Aunt Zura.'

Gina shook her head. 'She put us here. She might not want to help us escape.'

'We could try Uncle Sam,' said Friedel. 'He's got plenty of money. I bet he'd help us.'

Uncle Sam was married to Aunt Henne. Although their home was in Czestochowa, during the week he came to stay in Lodz, where he worked as an accountant.

Gina grinned. 'Perfect.'

'All right,' said Friedel. 'Let's do it.'

They wasted no time. When Gina got an idea in her head, she had to act on it right away. No doubts, no planning, no fears. But while Gina was adventurous, Friedel had strength and determination. If she set her mind on something, there was no changing it. Together, nothing could hold the sisters back.

The orphanage wasn't a prison, so they didn't need to break out. As soon as the day's school was over, they simply gathered their things and walked off. Friedel found the way to Uncle Sam's office, a dingy place filled with brown furniture and box files.

When they told him what they wanted, Uncle Sam was so surprised that his eyebrows shot to the top of his forehead. 'You're running away?'

'No,' said Friedel. 'We're going home.'

'But we haven't got any money for the train,' said Gina. 'Please, could you lend us a little? I'm sure Father will pay you back.'

'Hmph. With what, I wonder,' said Sam. 'Your papa, poor fellow, is broker than a beggar with a gas bill.'

'He will in the end, we promise.'

Sam wasn't convinced. 'And what of your family? You think they can house you and feed you? You'll be putting a burden on them, you know.'

The girls hadn't thought of this. In their eagerness it hadn't even crossed their minds that their parents and Martha were living in other people's homes, and that there was a good reason that Friedel, Gina and Bernard had been sent away.

But Friedel, although feeling a little ashamed, wouldn't give in. 'We just want to be with them. We can't stand it. *Please.*'

Their uncle grumbled a bit longer about how badly the girls were behaving, and how hard they'd be making things for their family. But in the end he fished out his wallet and withdrew a pair of blue banknotes. 'That should be enough to get you both to Czestochowa. Let's hope you grow up to have wisdom as great as your confidence. Because, right now, you are both very unwise.'

With a great many thank-yous and promises that Father really would pay him back, they left Uncle Sam to his files and papers. Freedom was beckoning.

Lodz railway station was a grand, ornate building in the centre of the city. Friedel and Gina walked into the concourse and gazed around, searching for any clues to where they should go. None of the Polish signs meant anything to them – it all just looked like weirdly spelled gibberish with far too many *y*'s and *z*'s. After some trial and error, they managed to find a station employee who spoke a little German and who helped them find the ticket counters. It didn't take long before they were running to the platform, excitedly clutching a pair of cheap one-way tickets to Czestochowa.

The train stood at the platform, a great gleaming beast hissing out clouds of steam, impatient to be off. The twins raced along the carriages, looking for one with room, and leapt in through the door just before a station guard slammed it shut. The engine churned, blotting out the station with gusts of smoke and steam, and began to move.

They were going home. Home was not a place any more. Home for Friedel and Gina was where Mum was, where Father and their brothers and sister were. Home was family now, wherever they happened to be.

The carriage seats were hard wooden benches, but the ride was a lot more comfortable than their last big train journey, the one that had brought them from Dusseldorf to Zbaszyn. Here they had room to breathe and windows

to look out of. They pressed their faces against the glass, trying to see ahead. What would the first glimpse of Czestochowa be like?

Kilometre after kilometre of Polish countryside sailed by. After about two hours, houses began to flit past on both sides, getting more and more tightly packed. Then big buildings, apartment blocks, factories, all hazed by the coal-smoke of a city. The train slowed and drew into a station. Friedel and Gina looked eagerly for a sign. And there it was:

Czestochowa

The twins left the station and took their first look at the place they'd heard so much about. The city of their ancestors.

Walking through the streets, the girls were excited but also nervous. In a way, they were coming back to where their family story had begun, years before they were born. There was joy in that. But Czestochowa was also a city wrapped up in dark ribbons of fear. This was the place from which Mum and Father had fled, taking Hans and baby Martha, to escape from people who were killing Jews. What fate might it hold for them now? And aside from all that, wouldn't Mum and Father be cross with them for running away from the orphanage?

As they walked, Friedel and Gina saw how beautiful Czestochowa was, and how extremely Catholic. At the end of the station road, they came to a great avenue. It was elegant, with two broad lanes for traffic either side and the middle lined with neat young trees – lindens and sycamores. In one direction, the avenue stretched away into the distance, rising up towards a huge building on a hill. It looked like a church, with a great spire reaching to the heavens.

The city was famous for this building. It held the Shrine of Our Lady of Czestochowa, which was well-known to Catholics. 'Our Lady' was, of course, none other than the twins' old acquaintance the Virgin Mary, Jesus's mum.

People came here on pilgrimages from all over Poland and beyond. The great tree-lined road leading up to it was named (take a deep breath) the Avenue of the Blessed Virgin Mary in Czestochowa.

Friedel and Gina's route took them in the opposite direction, towards the centre of the city. A little way along the avenue, they found themselves in a big open square, bustling with traffic and crowded with market stalls. This was the New Market, and it was here that Mum and Father were staying. Around the square were shops, each with a floor or two of apartments above them. It didn't look very different from the area around Marken Street in Dusseldorf.

When Mum answered the door, her jaw dropped. 'Friedel! Gina! What on earth are you doing here?'

'We've come home,' said Gina.

'Home! You're supposed to be in Lodz. How did you even *get* here?'

'Uncle Samuel gave us the money for the train,' said Friedel.

'Mum, we hated that orphanage,' said Gina. 'We had to leave.'

'Oh, you *had* to leave? As simple as that?'

'Well, yes,' said Gina.

Mum couldn't decide whether to be happy to see the girls, or just worried and angry. 'I don't know what we're going to do with you,' she said. 'There's no more space here, and Martha is staying at Aunt Henne's, so that's full up.'

Friedel and Gina were taken to Father, to tell him what they'd done, and to get a telling-off. Aunt Henne was asked what she thought, then other relations all gave their views on what to do with the twins. Nobody had space for them. The girls crossed their fingers and prayed they wouldn't be sent back to Lodz and the orphanage. Anything but that.

At last, after more relations had been asked, a room was discovered for them in another building in New Market. It would be large enough for the whole family.

It wasn't a particularly nice room. Not by any means. It was in a basement, and it was barely furnished and gloomy. A couple of high-up little windows looked out on the feet of people walking by in the market square. Beneath the basement were deep cellars lined with barrels where market traders stored their goods. They stank of fish and pickling vinegar.

The room had only a bed, a few chairs and a table, along with a cupboard to store the family's meagre belongings. Well, they'd lived in one room before – and had to share it with eleven other people – so they could do it again. Just like in Zbaszyn, they had no facilities for washing or doing laundry but they hoped it would only be for a short time. Once they got back on their feet they would have a proper home of their own.

The problem was money. All they'd had was the little bit of cash that Father had been allowed to bring from Germany, and that had long since run out. They still had belongings that they'd left behind in Dusseldorf, which Mr Wallach was taking care of for them. Mum and Father believed they could raise some money by selling them. But the question was, would they be able to get their things back?

After a lot of discussion and a great many headache-causing difficulties with the Polish and German authorities, it was settled. Mum decided that she would make the long trip to Dusseldorf and bring back whatever she could, leaving Father here to look after the family.

On a warm July day, Mum hugged her children and said goodbye, before boarding the train. It was a strange journey to be making – going to a place that had been home, but was now a foreign, hostile land. If she had known what was coming, she'd have hugged her children longer. Or perhaps not left at all.

The basement room was bleaker than ever without her presence. Father was getting more and more worried about the future, and especially about Martha. Would her health and strength stand up to the hardships they were facing – especially if things got worse? Max, who was nineteen now, had managed to leave Germany and was safe in England. Mum had relations there, in a place called Cheshire, and they were helping Max to settle in.

They were willing to help Martha as well, if she could manage to get there.

That was a very big *if*. Father was reluctant to let his most beloved daughter go, but at last he was persuaded. 'Think, Abraham,' his sister said. 'Once she's working over there, she'll be able to send money. And she can help get the other children to England.' Father had to agree. It would be best for everyone, especially for Martha herself.

But this was easier said than done. It was very hard for desperate Jews to get to safety in other countries. Many of the people in those countries didn't want refugees or immigrants. America was where most Jews wanted to go, but it was the country that seemed to want them the least. There were anti-refugee articles in newspapers and politicians made speeches against them, claiming that they would be a burden on the country, or even that they were dangerous. Only a tiny number of Jewish people managed to get together the money they needed to enter the country, and satisfied all the tricky rules America had for letting people in. But at this time – the summer of 1939 – Britain was making a special allowance for Jewish refugees, because some politicians and members of the public had campaigned to do more to help. As long as the would-be refugees could arrange a job for themselves before travelling to Britain, they were allowed to come. It was a very small gesture. There were few jobs on offer, and they

were all low-paid. All sorts of people, some of them highly educated men and women who'd once had good careers, advertised themselves in British newspapers, offering to be servants or cleaners or do any kind of work at all.

The Rosenthals' relations, together with Max, managed to sort this out for Martha. She was going to be a housemaid and nanny for a cousin of Mum's in London, which was a come-down from her old job with Mrs Boehrer. But the important thing was that it unlocked a door to a new life – a life where she could be safe.

* * *

On a Thursday in late July, with a fine summer warming the world, Martha set out alone on the greatest journey of her life. It made her deeply sad that Mum was still stuck in Dusseldorf, and that she wouldn't get to say goodbye.

Before departing, Martha left her doll, Leni, in Father's care. 'Give her to Friedel and Gina,' she said. 'They need her more than I do.'

Martha had to travel first to the city of Katowice,[*] where there was a British consulate (which is like an embassy but smaller). There she got her passport stamped with a visa, which gave her permission to go to Britain. The visa was quite expensive, and on top of that was the

---

[*] This is pronounced *Kat-o-veetza*.

cost of travelling all the way to Britain by train and ship. Uncle Sam was helping out with the costs, but it was a big stretch even for him.

From Katowice, Martha caught a train to the German border. That meant going back to Zbaszyn. The station and the town looked much the same as they had a short time ago when the Rosenthals were living here, but far quieter. With most of the refugees gone, the place felt almost deserted.

At the border, just beyond the edge of the town, the situation was tense. Many people feared that there might be a war soon between Germany and Poland.

There was a long history of Poland and its people being treated badly by Germany, going back long before the Nazis. It wasn't only the issue of the so-called *Volksdeutsche* – those Polish citizens who considered themselves German. There was also racism involved. Like many German leaders before him, Hitler believed that Poles had no real right to their own country. It wasn't only Jews that Hitler had extreme racist ideas about: he also thought that Polish people were lesser beings. They were white, mostly, but that didn't make them Aryan, and Hitler believed that their land should belong to Germany. Talks had been going on for months between the two countries, but they weren't going well.

Arriving in Zbaszyn, Martha went straight to German passport control at the border. The Nazi official stamped her passport and told her to report back later with all her necessary papers. She had three days to do so. If she was late, the stamp would expire.

This was simply Nazi spite against a Jewish girl; Martha already had all the papers she needed, but she still had to go away and come back. As it turned out, the obstinate border officers kept Martha waiting the whole three days before letting her through into Germany.

Martha was both scared and excited to be back. There was no question of going home to Dusseldorf. Instead she caught a train to Berlin, the capital city. From Berlin she would catch another train for the port city of Hamburg, where she would get on the ship for England.

She had a good friend who lived in Berlin, a Jewish girl called Ilse. They'd made friends at the special holiday place where Martha used to go to improve her health. Martha was sure Ilse would help her on her way.

It would have torn at Martha's heart to know that, while she had been waiting in Zbaszyn, a train had passed through going from Germany to Czestochowa, and on that train was Mum, returning from her trip.

It would have broken both their hearts if they had known that they would never have a chance to see or to hug one another again.

* * *

Mum's time in Dusseldorf had been stressful. Ever generous, Mr Wallach provided a roof over her head while she got together the family's precious belongings. There was far more than she could possibly carry alone, so she packed up most of it and arranged to have it transported by train to Czestochowa. As the days passed, Mum realised she didn't even know how she would afford the train fare back for herself. She had to beg and borrow whatever she could.

She made it back to Czestochowa just in time.

On 1 September 1939, exactly three weeks after Martha arrived in England, Nazi Germany launched their invasion of Poland.

* * *

The German forces swept into Poland like a tsunami – powerful, thundering forward at speed, impossible to resist. It was a new style of war, which the world of 1939 had never seen before. The Germans called it *Blitzkrieg* – 'lightning war' – and for anyone caught in its path, it was terrifying. Swarms of tanks smashed through the Polish defences, while dive-bombers came screaming from the sky and the ferocious Nazi soldiers killed everyone in sight.

Many of the Polish army units fought heroically, but it was hopeless, and many others simply retreated or were destroyed. The roads were filled with Polish people fleeing from the advancing storm. They piled their belongings into carts, wagons and cars, and tried desperately to escape.

People fled from the villages around Czestochowa, and for a day or two the city was clogged with the traffic passing through it. The Polish soldiers defending the city retreated, and some of the citizens joined the flood as it headed east, away from the Germans.

In their room in New Market, the Rosenthals could only sit tight and hope against hope that they would survive what was coming.

CHAPTER NINE

Things That Happen in War

It was ten o'clock on a quiet Sunday morning when the war arrived in Czestochowa. It rolled in along the roads in tanks and armoured vehicles. Military planes roared and droned in swarms in the skies above.

Alongside the tanks came thousands of German soldiers in their round helmets and grey uniforms. They held their rifles at the ready, some with machine guns on their shoulders trailing belts of bullets. The soldiers were watchful, but with the Polish garrison gone, nobody in the city tried to shoot at them or stop them. The streets were quiet. All the shops were shut, and many townsfolk had fled the day before.

All was peaceful.

At first it seemed to the Jews living in Czestochowa

that this might be a sign of hope. Perhaps the Nazis wouldn't be as ferocious as everyone had feared?

The German soldiers walked through the silent town, setting up their command posts. Sentries with machine guns guarded the main road junctions. But they didn't shoot or arrest anyone. They didn't even act in a menacing way. By midday, they had set up their headquarters in the town hall.

Nazi Germany now owned Czestochowa, and not a single shot had been fired.

But the Rosenthals knew all too well that if a Nazi seemed peaceful, that didn't mean you shouldn't be afraid. In their basement room, they waited to see what would happen. Friedel and Gina stood on chairs to peer out of the little window. Because it was at pavement level, it gave an ant's-eye view of the open space. New Market was a vast square – you could fit three football pitches into it and still have space left over. On market days it was a teeming hive of activity, with farmers arriving on their horse-drawn carts and tall, rickety hay wagons. Great fleets of them trundled in along the streets and lined up in the square. The sellers would then set up their stalls, dozens upon dozens of them in neat rows with colourful striped canopies. The whole square became a town in its own right, busy and noisy with shoppers buying, kids playing, horses snorting, and sellers shouting out to attract customers.

Today, though, the vast space was quiet, almost deserted. Only a tiny handful of people were out – those who had vital tasks to do, or whose curiosity was stronger than their caution. Where the farmers' carts usually parked, now there were a handful of German military vehicles. Where the shoppers and traders usually mingled, now the Nazi soldiers in their grey uniforms patrolled. Over it all, the elegant white front of St Zygmunt's church gazed out like a silent sentry.

More than anything else, one thing dominated the Rosenthals' thoughts. Somewhere, perhaps a long way from here, perhaps nearby, Hans must be with his regiment. Were they fighting still, or were they among the Polish troops that had been wiped out? Had they retreated? Was Hans still alive? What about his wife and their baby?

At least there was the comfort of knowing that Max was safe in England, and Martha too. She'd written to tell them she'd arrived, and had been given a job in London. There'd be little chance for her to send any money, because of the fighting. But at least she was out of danger.

* * *

On the day that the war arrived in Czestochowa, it was spreading out to the rest of the world as well.

That same Sunday, the governments of the United Kingdom and France declared war on Germany. They had given many warnings to Hitler before, and he had ignored them all. The year before, he'd taken over Austria

and invaded part of Czechoslovakia,* and the world had done nothing about it. But in invading Poland, Hitler crossed a line. Britain and France would not put up with his behaviour any longer.

They were all but alone in making a stand, at least for the time being. A few of Britain's Commonwealth friends, such as Australia and Canada, were quick to join in, but most other countries were not willing to help. The most powerful of them, the United States, stayed out of it. America saw it as Europe's war, and therefore Europe's problem. They turned a blind eye to Hitler's evil acts and carried on doing business with Nazi Germany. Perhaps the world cared about Poland and its people; perhaps they cared about the Jews. But not as much as they cared about making money and staying out of trouble.

The Second World War had begun, but for the time being, most of the world sat on the sidelines and watched to see how it would unfold.

* * *

In Czestochowa, the rest of that Sunday carried on quietly. People rested, the braver ones went out to church, and some carried on living their lives as normal. If you

---

* Czechoslovakia is now two separate countries – the Czech Republic (also known as Czechia) and Slovakia.

ignored all the tanks and guns and German uniforms, it could almost have been a typical Sunday.

When Monday morning dawned, everything was still peaceful. The German soldiers seemed to have got their bearings and had started being friendly to the townsfolk. Some of them even handed out biscuits and chocolate.

But not all the soldiers were so relaxed. There had been rumours of Polish fighters lurking in buildings to ambush them, which made some of the German soldiers tense. They didn't give out food. Instead they kept their hands on their guns and watched the windows of the nearby houses for any suspicious signs.

The bells of the city's churches rang out for one o'clock. The chimes of the Church of St Zygmunt clanged through the great open space of New Market, and across the Old Market square, which lay on the other side of the church.

As the metallic echoes died away, the first gunshot snapped through the air. A loud, resounding *crack!*

Then came another shot from a different street, then more and more, and more still. They seemed to come from all directions – *Crack! Crack! Crack-ack-ack!* And then came the distinctive, awful noise of German machine guns, which was like a tearing sheet.

Nobody knew what was going on. Who was shooting? The obvious answer was that it must be German soldiers, but who were they shooting at, and why? It was as if the war had been holding its breath, and now let it out in a resounding blast that ripped through Czestochowa's streets and squares.

In their basement room, the Rosenthals stared at each other in dismay and fear. Had the Polish army returned to liberate the city? Had the Nazis started killing Jews? Father sat in his chair, listening intently. Friedel and Gina, with Bernard alongside, looked out through the little window, but there was nothing to be seen from here. The shooting seemed to be coming from beyond New Market – at a guess, it sounded like most

of it came from over towards Strazacka Street, a couple of blocks away.

Suddenly the gunfire broke out in New Market itself. There were screams, and a handful of people came running across the square. Then came German soldiers, shooting at the people. It wasn't the Polish army liberating the city, and it wasn't resistance fighters. The German soldiers were murdering civilians. Right in front of St Zygmunt's church they rounded them up and gunned them down.

'Come away from the window!' Mum shouted.

Friedel, Gina and Bernard were glued to the grimy little pane of glass, appalled but unable to stop watching. Mum's voice cut through the spell, and they jumped down from their perch, shaking with horror.

The shooting went on and on, in isolated bursts around the district. When it finally stopped, over a thousand people lay dead in the streets.

Nobody knew what was going on. Even the Germans were confused, and the soldiers now shooting at civilians didn't really know why they were doing it.

Afterwards, once calm had been restored, people began to learn what had happened. The Germans claimed that Polish fighters had shot at them from houses in Strazacka Street. But that claim was false. In truth, some soldiers had fired their guns by mistake, thinking they saw the flash of gunfire. It was probably just sunlight glinting on windows. Then other soldiers joined in, and soon they were all panicking. The confusion of terror made them see imaginary enemies everywhere. Some even shot at each other. The chaos had turned into a wave of murderous madness.

The Jewish people of Czestochowa believed that the Nazis were acting on their hatred of Jews, but it wasn't so. Many Jews had been shot, but by far most of the dead were non-Jewish Polish people.

Still, it was a taste of what the Nazis could do when the madness took hold of them.

CHAPTER TEN

The District of Doomed Souls

1940

A year went by in Czestochowa, and people got used to their new reality. Another summer came, bright and hot as Polish summers often are.

Friedel walked through the park, across the river from the city centre, pushing a pram. Inside was a sleeping baby. She looked around contentedly at the trees and greenery of the park. Sycamores, drooping green willows and copper beeches were scattered about across the grass and lined the paths. On such a fine summer's day, Friedel could almost forget the events of recent years, and imagine that she was still a little child, playing in the Grafenberger Forest. So much had changed, so many terrible events had happened, that it seemed like a different world. Even so, those memories were as fresh in her mind as the day they were made.

The pram wheels squealed gently as she pushed it along. She looked down at the baby. The bright blue eyes in the crinkled face opened and darted curiously about. The baby wasn't hers, of course. Friedel was sixteen – not far off being a grown-up, but still a very long way from wanting babies of her own. The baby's mother, Mrs Kozak, was a very busy woman. She had a shop selling women's hats, and employed Friedel to look after the baby.

With the Germans in charge, life for Jews in Czestochowa wasn't much worse than it had been in Dusseldorf. At least, not at first. In some ways it was actually better. People like Mrs Kozak were still allowed to own businesses and shops. Jews could go about the city freely, and even travel if they could afford it.

But in every other way, life was terrible, and as time passed it kept on getting worse. There wasn't much work for Jews, and most were going hungry, having to sell off their belongings for food. There was humiliation too. All Jews had to wear a clear mark to show that they were Jewish. This took the form of a white armband embroidered with a blue Star of David – the symbol of Jewishness. The Nazis had evicted many hundreds of Jews from their homes in the posher parts of the city and forced them to find places to live in the older, poorer area near the river. The streets around New Market and Old Market were now officially the Jewish district.

It had its own council to run things. The Nazis had set up a committee they called the *Judenrat*, meaning 'Jewish Council'. It was made up of people from the Jewish community, and its job was to oversee the goings-on in their district, and report back to the Nazi authorities. The people who were in the Jewish Council were, in effect, helping the Nazis. They had many reasons for doing so. Some felt that it was the best way to keep the city's Jewish people safe. Some perhaps believed that it was the best way to keep themselves and their own families safe. They reported on everything: how many people were living there, their names, the jobs they did, and any problems they were having or causing.

There weren't nearly enough houses or apartments, so people had to crowd in with other families. Once again the Rosenthals found themselves sharing their only room with a lot of strangers, just like in Zbaszyn.

For Friedel, looking after Mrs Kozak's baby was a way of making a little bit of money. But it also helped her to escape from the misery for a short time each day. She would push the pram across the bridge to Narutowicza* park, which lay beside the river, on the bank opposite the Jewish district. It was a pretty park, filled with wandering

---

* This is pronounced *Na-root-o-veecha*.

paths and trees. The city was hidden from view, along with all its unpleasantness.

Today was especially nice – a glorious August afternoon, warm and cheerful. Friedel parked the pram and unfurled a blanket on the dry, crackling grass. Laying the baby down, she sat and closed her eyes, feeling the sun on her face.

Bliss. Just for a moment – a precious, rare moment – she could almost believe that the world was good.

Friedel's bubble of contentment was popped suddenly by a distant scream, a faint, high-pitched shriek from somewhere across the river. She opened her eyes, sitting bolt upright, listening. Another distant shout, and another yell of terror.

She jumped to her feet and ran across the grass verge, over the path, and through a patch of trees to the river's edge. Across the water, somewhere among the city streets, the shouts and screams were growing louder. It sounded like a riot breaking out. Her mind shot back to that awful day when the Nazis massacred all those people. From there her thoughts leapt to her family. Whatever was going on over there, they were right in the middle of it.

Friedel sprinted back to the baby, snatching him up in her arms and laying him in the pram, bundled up in his blanket. Then she ran, the pram wheels squealing wildly, along the winding path, out of the park, over the bridge, plunging back into the Jewish district.

The screams and shouts grew louder. She could see people running at the far end of the street, with German soldiers chasing them. Panic was rising in Friedel's throat. She longed to go home to see if her family were safe, but she had to see to the baby first.

Racing through the streets, doubling back now and then to avoid the soldiers, she made it to the Kozaks' house. Without bothering to knock, she pushed open the front door, struggling to get the pram up the step and into the hallway.

There was no sight or sound of anyone. 'Hello?' she called out. 'Mrs Kozak?'

No answer. Friedel ran from room to room, but nobody was there.

Grabbing as many baby things as she could – bottle, nappies, a couple of toys – she stuffed them into the

pram and hurried back out into the street. The baby's grandparents lived nearby. She decided to head there.

The turmoil was growing a little quieter, but that wasn't a good thing. It simply meant that most of the people running away had been caught. The only shouts now were in German – orders yelled out angrily. Friedel saw Nazi soldiers rounding up groups of young Jewish men at gunpoint, marching them along. They appeared to be heading in the direction of Warsaw Market, which was at the top end of the Jewish district.

To Friedel's huge relief, the grandparents were at home, and Mrs Kozak was with them.

'My darling!' she said as she took the baby in her arms. 'You're safe! Thank you, Friedel, I knew he'd be safe with you. Now run along. Go to your people, and be careful!'

Friedel didn't need telling twice. She was back out in the street almost before Mrs Kozak had finished speaking. Taking care to avoid the German soldiers, she hurtled along the pavement, round a corner, and back to New Market.

Down in the basement, Friedel was overjoyed to find her parents safe. They'd guessed she must be out with the baby, and had been worried sick. Mum hugged her.

'What in the world is going on out there?' she said.

Friedel told them what she'd heard and seen. At first, nobody knew what it meant. They found out later that the young men who'd been rounded up were being sent away to a camp at a place in Poland named Belzec.* The Nazis called it a labour camp, but really it was a *forced* labour camp, and the men there lived – and many died – in terrible conditions.

The Jewish Council had helped to organise the round-up by making a list of all the young men who were fit to work. People in the district hated the Council almost as much as they hated the Nazis. Hated them more, perhaps. There was even a Jewish police force now. Run by the Jewish Council, it helped to enforce the Nazis' laws against the Jews. Folk in the district despised these police too, seeing them as traitors to their own people. How could they do such a thing? It was beyond shameful.

By now, Jewish people all over Germany, Austria, Poland, and everywhere the Nazis invaded had seen so many terrible things that it was hard to keep hope alive. They had learned that things could always get worse. The only question was – how much worse, and how soon?

For the Rosenthal family, the answer to that question was not long in coming. There were more round-ups of young men for the labour camp, and one of those the Nazis took was Bernard.

He was still only seventeen, but he was herded together with the others at gunpoint, marched to Warsaw

---

* This is pronounced *Bel-zhetz*.

Market, and taken away. There was no chance even to say goodbye. It was hard to imagine that any of the boys and men who were sent to Belzec would ever be seen again.

The twins had lost their one remaining brother, and their parents were grief-stricken, especially Mum. She now had to worry about Bernard as well as Hans. Both were far away, beyond her reach, and both were in terrible danger.

News came from Hans, but it did little to calm the family's fears. Through luck and daring, he had managed to survive the German invasion. He had escaped from Poland just ahead of the Nazi tidal wave, and made it to the Soviet Union – the empire ruled by Russia. The family had received a letter from him in February. He'd managed to take his wife with him, and they were now living in the city of Mogilev. But they were in dreadful poverty, and there was nothing the family could do to help.

It was more than Mum could bear. Now that Bernard was gone too, she began to cherish the things he had left behind, as if it would somehow keep him close to her.

* * *

A harsh Polish winter came and went, bitterly cold and fraught with starvation. Bread was rationed, and supplies were so short that Gina would go out at two o'clock in the morning to queue up for the ration. She had to stand for hours in the bitter cold. Poles would push in ahead of the Jews, calling them names and shoving them out of the way.

The following spring, the Nazis decided that Jews needed to be controlled even more severely. So they turned the Jewish district into something they called a *ghetto*.

'Ghetto' is an old word. It was invented hundreds of years ago by Italians in Venice. Ghetto was their name for the part of their city where Jews were made to live. In the centuries that followed, it came to mean the part of any city where all the Jews lived, sometimes by choice, usually by law.* The Nazis were extremely keen on ghettos for Jewish people, and they created them in most of Poland's cities.

The order was given that all Jews must move into the area that would become the ghetto and all Poles must move out of it. The Nazis then set boundaries. It was a small area, with New Market and Old Market at its centre, and just two or three blocks on each side. By the time the move was complete, there were around 28,000 Jewish people living within this handful of streets and squares. More were moved in from other smaller towns, and within a year the number would grow to nearly fifty

---

* Sometimes it refers to other ethnic minorities, but it is mostly connected with Jewish areas.

thousand. Nobody was allowed to enter or leave without permission from the Nazis.

Most of the ghettos made by the Nazis in Poland had high barbed wire fences round them. But Czestochowa had no fence. The Nazis here apparently believed that fear of punishment was enough to keep people in.

All around, the police kept their eyes open for anyone disobeying. The Polish police worked for the Nazis now. They were known as the 'Blue Police' because of their uniforms, distinct from the grey of the Germans.

At first the punishment for leaving the ghetto was a hefty fine and perhaps prison. Soon that changed to

something far more severe. Signs were put up on the streets leading out of the ghetto, warning that any Jew straying outside the boundary would be killed. On the outside were signs making the same threat against any Poles caught entering the ghetto.

There would be no more visits to the park for Friedel. No more life, really, other than what she and Gina could invent for themselves. From now on, their existence would become a grim game, where the prize was life itself and the penalty for losing was death.

* * *

Out in the world beyond, the war had been raging on for nearly two years. France had surrendered. Most of western Europe was now either controlled by Nazi Germany or allied to it. Only Britain and the Commonwealth countries, helped out by men and women who'd escaped from Nazi-occupied Europe, were still fighting.

Then, a few months after the ghetto in Czestochowa began, the war suddenly grew much, much larger.

In June 1941, Hitler invaded the Soviet Union. The Soviet Union was Russia's empire, and it was vast. Unimaginably huge. Accordingly, Hitler sent a massive military force to try to conquer it. Millions of soldiers, together with thousands of planes and tanks, attacked all along Russia's border. It was another Blitzkrieg. But it wasn't as successful as the ones against Poland or France. Although huge numbers of Soviet troops were wiped out or captured, the Soviet lands were so enormous that Russia was continuing to fight back, retreating, regrouping, and refusing to give up.

For the Rosenthals, the news redoubled their worries about Hans. Mogilev, which was on the western edge of the Soviet Union, was one of the first cities captured by the Nazi forces. The Rosenthals had no idea what had become of Hans or his wife, and no way of finding out. They could only fear the worst.

In December, the miracle that people in Europe had been praying for finally arrived. America joined the war at last – on Britain's side, of course. Japan, which was an ally of Nazi Germany, had attacked the American navy at a place called Pearl Harbor in the Pacific Ocean. Hitler jumped at the chance to declare war on the United States. He admired America for its industry and power. Also, the racist way the country treated Black people had helped inspire the Nazi laws against Jews. But he also despised the American people. He thought they were degenerate in things like art and music and personal freedom. He also knew that America's army was far smaller than Germany's. He was sure they'd be crushed by his military might. As with so many of Hitler's ideas, this belief could not have been more wrong.

The Second World War had now truly lived up to its name, engulfing the whole planet in conflict.

CHAPTER ELEVEN

Blackbirds and Morphine

1942

Gina crouched, still as a blackbird, eyes roving over the street below. She was perched high on a rooftop overlooking Mirowska Street. This was one of the main avenues leading out of the ghetto, and it was heavily patrolled by the Jewish police. Gina could see a couple of them, with their caps and shiny badges and their air of self-importance.

The weather was hot, even for August. Poland can be extremely warm in summer and bitterly cold in winter. But up on the roof, the air was breezy and a little cooler than in the street.

Gina took her harmonica from her pocket, and picked some bits of fluff from the holes. It would be nice to play up here, but did she dare risk making a sound?

Yes, she dared. Blowing softly, she teased an old Jewish tune from the instrument. It floated on the air, lifting her spirits.

There was a skitter of feet on the tiles, and Gina turned to see Friedel scuttling up to join her on the high point.

'What took you so long?' said Gina.

'Tricky climb,' Friedel replied.

The rooftops had become their sanctuary, and the route they used to move around the ghetto. It was the only sure way of avoiding harassment from the Jewish police. The apartment buildings were all joined together in blocks, so if you could climb up to the rooftops it was easy to pass from one street to another.

It also helped them to run a scheme they'd cooked up, to keep themselves and their family from starvation. It was strictly against the law, and needed the utmost caution and secrecy.

Friedel no longer worked for Mrs Kozak. Instead she had a job helping out in a grocery supplies shop. Even before the Nazis shut everyone into the ghetto, food and other supplies were extremely difficult to get hold of. Friedel suspected that the man who employed her traded on the black market, which meant he bought and sold goods that had been stolen from somewhere – like a factory, a warehouse, or perhaps a parked van. She guessed that the goods were smuggled into the ghetto by Polish traders.

Taking advantage of the situation, Friedel pocketed small items: soap, coffee, vegetables, sausages, or whatever she could lay hands on. Meanwhile, Gina had found a job in a bakery, and she would steal a few rolls or a loaf of bread. Carrying their spoils, the girls would head to the rooftops to rendezvous. In the early days, before the ghetto began, they used to meet up with Bernard, who brought the food back to their parents. After the Nazis took Bernard, the girls had to manage the loot by themselves.

What they were doing was a crime, of course, and would be severely punished if they were caught. But although they feared the punishment, they weren't sorry about the crime. They felt they had a duty to help their family to survive, and that duty was more important than anything else. Compared to seeing their mother and father starve, any other questions of right and wrong didn't seem very important to the sisters.

Crouched beside Gina, Friedel looked down on Mirowska Street. Just a little way along was the bridge leading to Narutowicza park, and at one edge of the bridge a checkpoint, where police watched for anyone entering or leaving the ghetto. She missed the greenery. There were very few trees and hardly any grass at all

within the ghetto, and Friedel ached for the freedom she had lost.

'Better get moving,' said Gina, handing her bag of bread to Friedel.

Friedel looked inside. 'What, no cream cakes?' she said with a grin.

'Away with you,' said Gina. 'I've got to get back to work.'

They moved quickly across the roof, the clay tiles clinking under their boots.

Gina was an expert at this – she and Bernard used to love climbing on the building sites back in Dusseldorf.

But Friedel had become skilled too, and both girls could scurry over the rooftops like cats, up and down a drainpipe or a ladder, in through an open loft window, or down a handy fire escape. Often they crept into an apartment or a shop storeroom and scavenged whatever bits of food they could find.

Back on the ground, they parted ways. As Gina headed for the bakery, Friedel went round the corner to New Market, and ran across the square to their building.

Down in the basement, she found Mum and Father waiting. The heat down here was stifling. The room was crowded, with each family or couple or stray individual inhabiting their own tiny bit of space. There was no ventilation, and the air was humid with the body-warmth of a dozen people.

Mum sat in her chair, sewing by the light of a candle. She was no longer the same mother Friedel remembered from the old days. Hunger had taken away her chubby, cheerful features, and the skin round her eyes was lined from constant stress.

Father lay on the small bed, dozing fitfully, his face glistening with sweat. He woke up as Friedel came in, gazing at her with groggy, pale eyes. 'Who is that?' he murmured.

'It's me, Father.' She settled down between her parents and discreetly showed Mum the contents of her bags.

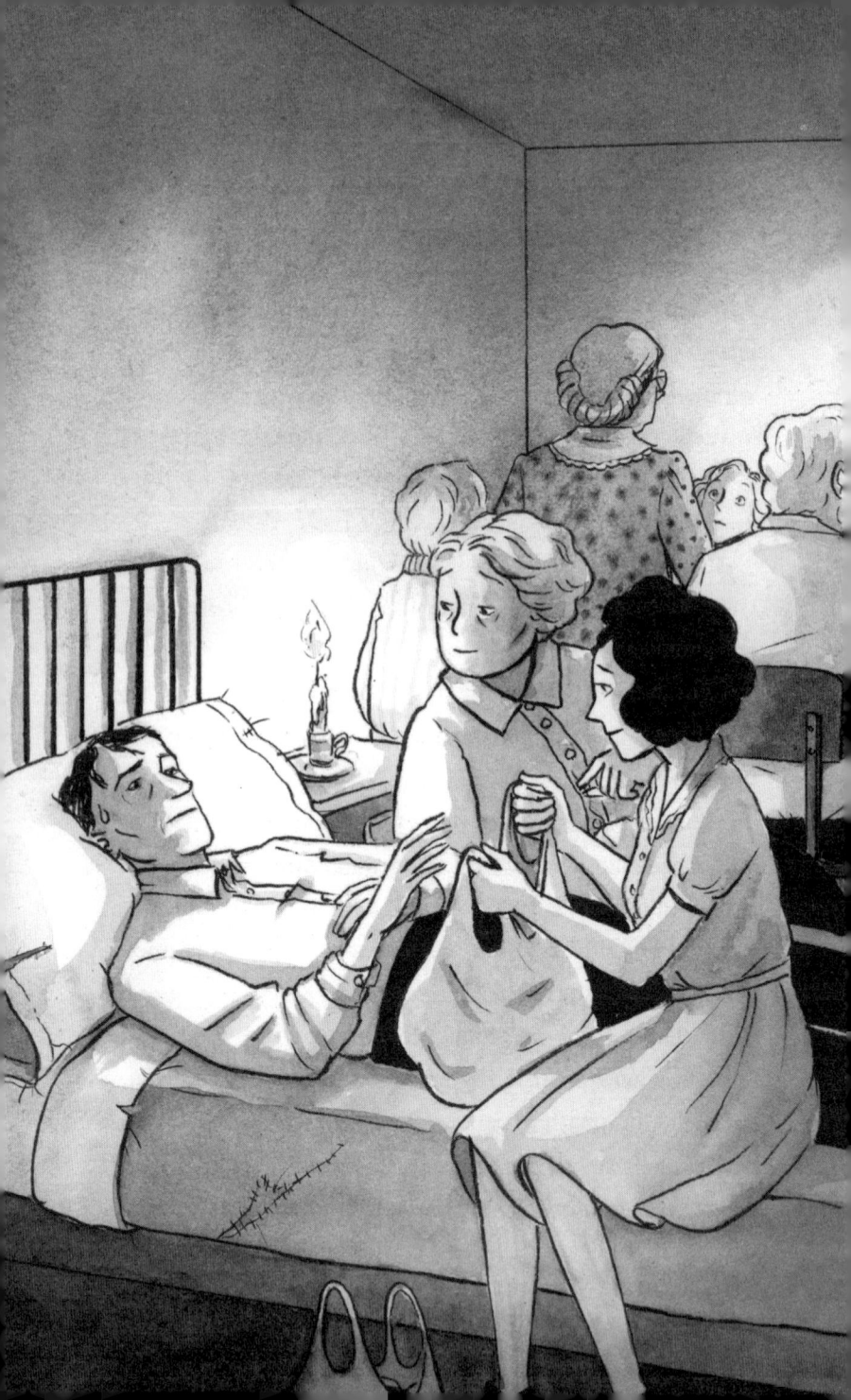

Mum nodded, and gave the faintest ghost of a smile. 'Good girls. Look, Abraham,' she whispered. 'Friedel's brought food.'

Father came fully awake and looked in the bags. He didn't approve of stealing, no matter what the circumstances. He had a very strong sense of what was proper. And besides, running a shop would give anyone a loathing of theft. But he didn't say anything – he knew his girls were not really thieves. They were just loving daughters trying to do the best for their family.

'Won't you eat, Abraham?' said Mum. 'Just a little?' Father shook his head and touched his belly.

He wasn't well. Not well at all. He'd been getting more and more ill lately with stomach pain. It wasn't indigestion, and it wasn't appendicitis. Although he and Mum tried to keep their thoughts secret from the kids, they suspected it was something much more serious. But they couldn't be sure, and it was all but impossible to find out. The ghetto had its own little hospital, just for Jews. But like most people, Father was frightened of going there. Those who did were often sent away by the Nazis and never seen again. What happened to them didn't bear thinking about.

Friedel's stomach twinged in sympathy, like an echo of the appendicitis she'd had years before. She couldn't imagine having to suffer an aching belly like that every day, with little hope of getting better. There must be *something* she could do to help him, mustn't there? She went out, closing the door softly behind her, and headed back to work.

* * *

When the sisters came home that evening, Father was still lying on the bed, doubled up in pain. Mum sat beside him, holding his hand. Her eyes were filled with fear as she looked up at the two girls.

'It's getting worse,' she said.

'Isn't there anything we can give him?' asked Gina.

'I think he needs morphine,' said Mum.

Morphine is an extremely strong painkiller – just about any pain, no matter how agonising, can be soothed by it. But it is hard to get, especially for Jews in a Nazi-controlled ghetto. 'We'll have to get the doctor,' Mum added.

Father's eyes opened in bleary terror at the word. 'No,' he muttered. 'No doctor. No hospital.'

Mum squeezed his hand to comfort and reassure him. It hurt the twins deeply to see their parents suffer like this. The two of them went and sat down in a corner of the room.

'We have to do something,' said Gina. 'There must be *something* we can do to help. Something we can . . . you know, pinch.'

'The grocer's doesn't run to morphine, Gina. And I doubt if the bakery does either.'

Gina had no answer to that. 'But there must be *something*,' she said lamely.

They fell silent.

Some people near them were talking – a young woman was trying to reassure her mother.

'But they did it in Lublin,' the older woman was saying. 'Why not here?' Her eyes, glittering in the candlelight, were wide with terror.

Friedel and Gina both knew what the old woman was talking about. Even with the restrictions on the ghetto, news trickled in from outside. Earlier that year, the Nazis had destroyed the ghetto in the city of Lublin. They called it 'liquidation'. The Jews living there had been rounded up and sent away to concentration camps.

These were special camps that had been created by the Nazis to hold all the people they saw as enemies. The first concentration camp had been set up within weeks of Hitler coming to power, in 1933. Now there were hundreds of them. At first they held political enemies of the Nazis, as well as many others who the Nazis believed were a bad influence on Germany, such as gay and transgender people. Anyone with a disability was removed from society too. Since 1938, more and more Jews had been sent to the camps. Roma people – travellers, also known as gypsies – were despised by the Nazis too, and they received the same treatment. Jewish and Roma people were now being sent to a special new type of concentration camp, known as a death camp. There were rumours that when people reached these camps they were all killed with poison gas. Most people didn't believe this – or didn't want to believe it. Many felt that such a thing was too terrible even for the Nazis. They were wrong. The rumours were true.

'We'll be all right,' said the old woman's daughter. 'Maybe the liquidation won't happen in Czestochowa.'

The twins didn't know what to think. They were as scared as anyone, but their thoughts right now were focused on their parents.

Father settled down after a while, and they all gradually fell asleep to the sound of his troubled breathing and the surrounding murmurs and snores of the room's other inhabitants.

* * *

Friedel gazed up at the gloomy face of the apartment building in front of her. The summer night wasn't too dark to make out the rusty drainpipe snaking crookedly up the brickwork to the gutter high above.

She wasn't even supposed to be out of doors. The ghetto was under a permanent curfew – which meant that nobody was allowed out of their homes in the evening or at night. Friedel was risking everything just by being here. That made the rooftops all the more enticing as a way of getting about.

Bracing herself, Friedel gripped the iron drainpipe and started to climb. But it was almost rusted through, and began to pull away from the bricks before she'd climbed more than a couple of metres.

She dropped back to the pavement and looked for another way up. There was a broken window round the corner, leading to a stairwell. She climbed through, snagging her dress on the jagged edges of the glass, then went softly up the stairs. The building was filled with the sounds of people – the clank of cooking pots and chink of plates, as families did their best to make a meal with what scraps they had.

At the top of the stairs, Friedel found a skylight with a broken catch. Hauling herself up, at last she found herself on the roof. She felt at home in the familiar landscape of tiles and chimney pots – and oh, the sweet, wonderful fresh air! But she couldn't spare the time to relish it right now. She was on an urgent mission.

Making her way quickly but cautiously across the tiles, she went up over the ridge and down the other side. Looking down on the next street, she could only make out vague shadows in the moonlight. Nobody seemed to be about, not even the police.

Adjusting the bag slung over her shoulder, Friedel began heading along the roof towards the corner of the building. The tiles were uneven, and she had to take care. One false step or one loose tile could mean a swift and fatal fall to the pavement far below.

She found another skylight and descended to the landing inside. She scurried quickly down the stairs. On the ground floor, she paused in the hallway before softly opening the front door and glancing out. Still quiet, still no signs of movement.

Friedel crept out of the door and, looking furtively around her, ran across the street to the shadows on the far corner. Then, along a little way, she came to Dr Gruenberg's building. She slipped inside and found the room where he and his family lived. She knocked.

The door was opened by the doctor himself. He looked weary and stressed. There weren't many doctors left in the ghetto now – most of the young ones had been sent away to the labour camps along with the other young men. Visits at all hours of the day and night from folk begging for help were a common event for Dr Gruenberg. It was heartbreaking, and all the more so because he could do so little for them.

Taking one look at Friedel's face, he braced himself for the worst. 'How may I help you?'

Friedel's words came out in a rush. 'It's my father, sir. His stomach – pain in his stomach. It's awful. My mother says he needs morphine. Do you have any? Can you let me have some?'

'Slow down, girl! What is the ailment? Do you know?'

'He hasn't seen a doctor. He's scared of the hospital.'

Dr Gruenberg sighed. Everyone was scared of the hospital and only the most desperate went there. He listened as Friedel described her father's symptoms and how long it had been going on. His face became grave, frowning deeply. It sounded extremely serious.

'I can't come now. The curfew, you know. Give me your address. I shall try to call in and see him tomorrow morning.' He paused, then said, 'There will be a fee to pay, you understand? I have a family of my own to care for; you must know that.'

Friedel nodded. She'd expected this.

The doctor began to close the door. 'Tomorrow morning, then. Goodnight.'

Friedel pushed against the door, stopping it from closing. 'Please, he needs something now. I can't stand seeing him suffer like this. Can you give me morphine?'

Dr Gruenberg stared at her in astonishment. Friedel held his stare without flinching. 'I can pay. Here, look.'

She opened her bag and showed him the contents – a small packet of coffee and a couple of cans of vegetables.

The doctor's eyes narrowed. 'I know you,' he said. 'You work in the grocer's. I've seen you there.' He pressed his lips together, hesitating as he looked at the precious articles in Friedel's bag. 'Oh, very well then. Wait there.'

He went back inside, leaving the door ajar. When he reappeared a few minutes later, he held out a small glass bottle to Friedel. In the dim light she read the label: *Morphine sulphate 15mg*. Two white pills rattled inside it.

'Give him one tonight,' said the doctor. 'Just the one, mark you. Another in the morning. Then I will call.'

Friedel handed him the goods from the bag. 'Thank you, doctor.'

It was a quick journey back across the rooftops. In the basement, Friedel showed the bottle to Mum. 'Look, I got them!'

Mum's frown melted briefly into a smile, and she hugged Friedel. Taking out one of the pills, Mum handled it as if it were a precious nugget of gold. She offered it to Father. He opened his mouth and she slipped it in gently. He took a drink of water from the jug, then settled back.

It took a while for the tablet to work, but when it did, the effect was astonishing. Morphine doesn't only send the pain away – it gives a feeling of almost heavenly bliss. This makes it dangerous, because people can quickly become addicted to it.

Father's face relaxed for the first time in weeks. He

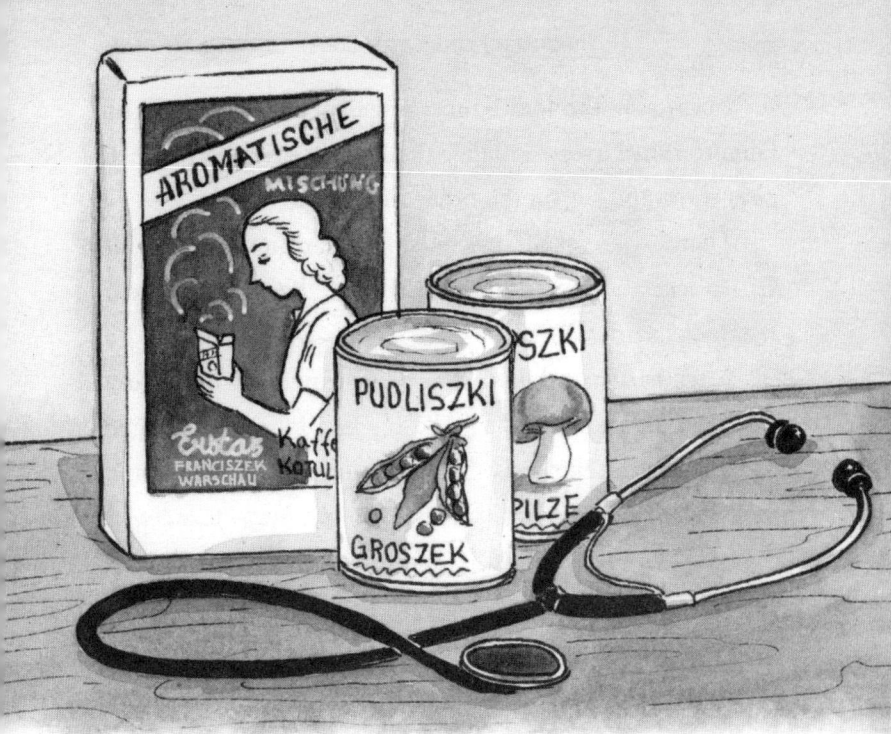

opened his eyes and smiled at Mum and at his daughters. 'Thank you,' he murmured.

Then, gradually, he fell into a deep, restful sleep.

* * *

Dr Gruenberg came the next morning, as he'd promised. Father's pain had returned. Mum was saving the other precious pill until he could no longer bear it.

As he examined the patient, the doctor's face hardened. He was accustomed to giving bad news, and he was now preparing himself to deliver the worst news possible.

Mum saw the look, and she gestured to Friedel and Gina to move away and give them some privacy. The two girls went and sat on the other side of the room.

There was a soft-voiced conversation between Dr Gruenberg and their parents. Although they couldn't hear what was said, they could tell it was bad.

After the doctor had left, they wanted to ask Mum what he'd said, but the look on her face discouraged them. Even so, the girls weren't children any more, and they believed they could guess what it was. Cancer. If that was so, then even if Father did go to the hospital, its meagre facilities wouldn't be able to help.

Over the following weeks, Friedel made the perilous journey over the roofs to Dr Gruenberg's several more times, trading stolen groceries for morphine. His supply was limited, though, and it could only help Father sleep in comfort. It couldn't save him or make his pain go away altogether.

On a day near the end of August, when the summer heat was at its most intense, the cancer finally took Father away from them. At last he was at peace, free of his pain, free of the anxiety and misery. But his family were not yet freed from theirs.

CHAPTER TWELVE

A World Full of Sledgehammers

Friedel and Gina had only one dress each. Their others had been sold to pay for food, along with all the family's best clothes. Their remaining garments were worn constantly, and always in need of repair. Now the girls learned that their only dresses must be dyed black, for Father's funeral.

There was little time to do it. In Jewish tradition, funerals are not delayed and, if possible, must happen within a day of the person dying.

A sheet had been draped over Father's body. Wearing their hastily dyed dresses, Friedel and Gina sat beside the bed, watching over him. Mum sat with them. There was a look in her eyes as if something in her had died too.

At last a rabbi came to conduct the funeral. He greeted Mum and the girls solemnly. As he gave his blessing, he motioned the three of them to stand. Friedel knew what was coming. When a close family member dies, it is traditional for a Jewish person to make a cut or a tear in their clothing. This is called *kriah*. It is supposed to show that your grief is so deep that you have torn your garment in anguish. In normal times, you would probably put on one of your less valuable pieces of clothing. The Rosenthals had no such thing.

The rabbi produced a small pair of scissors. Friedel tensed as he reached up and made a small cut on the left side of her dress's neckline. She knew what she was supposed to do now – tear the dress where he'd made the cut. The rabbi frowned at her as she hesitated. Then, forcing herself, she ripped the material. Gina did the same to hers, then Mum took her turn.

After the ritual was over, they waited for the men to come and carry Father's body to the burial ground. When they arrived at last, Mum and the girls followed behind and stood in silence as the rabbi gave the service of burial.

They each had their own memories of Father, from long ago, before the world turned bad. The bicycle trips to the Grafenberger Forest, pausing in the glades to pick fruit ... The dejected look on his face as they all spurned his vegetarian food and tucked into their chicken soup ... Standing proudly by the shop counter, wrapped in the aromas of coffee and fresh tobacco ... Angrily fetching Friedel from her hiding place in the bathroom ... Watching with adoring pride as Martha pedalled her first bike ... Surrounded by his family on a bright summer's day picnic ... Listening in rapture to his beloved operas ...

As they walked back to the basement, Friedel was lost in her own thoughts. Despite all she had been through, she had never experienced the death of someone she loved. It left her feeling afraid. Frightened for herself, for Gina, and above all for Mum. Suddenly, without

Father's strong, protective presence, they felt exposed and horribly fragile, like china cups in a world full of sledgehammers.

* * *

Less than a month had passed since Father's funeral. Just before first light on a September morning, the Nazis dropped one of those sledgehammers on the Czestochowa ghetto.

Yom Kippur had taken place the day before – the holiest of all holy days to Jewish people, that day when it is said that God writes down and seals each person's fate in the Book of Life. The Nazis chose this moment to enact the very thing the Jews had lived in fear of for months: the liquidation of the ghetto.

Even before Yom Kippur, frightening rumours had been whispered around the ghetto. People claimed that a Nazi 'liquidation squad' had come to Czestochowa and was waiting somewhere outside the boundary. It was said too that the members of the Jewish Council had left the ghetto for their own safety.

As people lit candles on the evening of the holy day, the whole ghetto was filled with prayers and fear. The Jews of Czestochowa were about to discover that every dreadful tale they'd heard from the Lublin ghetto was true.

In the streets outside, the Nazi police formed a cordon, cutting off any possible escape routes. So began the '*Aktion*'* as the Nazis called it.

Squads went inside the ghetto and started rounding up the Jews. They began in the northern section, a couple of streets away from New Market. The police called out through loudhailers, ordering everyone out into the street. Some people tried to hide, but most were forced

---

* This German word can mean *action*, but in this case it means *operation* or *mission*.

outside, where the police chased and beat them. Men, women and children began to panic, rushing through the street.

Huddled in their basement room, Friedel, Gina and Mum could hear the distant noises. The bile of fear rose in their throats. Every moment, they expected the shouting and panic to come nearer, find them, chase them out.

Minutes ticked by. They began to hear shooting. Not just occasional random shots but loud, crashing barrages of gunfire. It sounded a long way off. As the minutes grew into hours, still the noise grew no closer. Gradually it died down. Night began to fall, yet nobody came to get them. Outside the little window, New Market was quiet, and all but empty.

What was going on? Was it too much to hope that the liquidation had been stopped? If so, why?

The liquidation had not been stopped. The truth became clear over the following days. The ghetto, with its thousands upon thousands of inhabitants, was far too much for the Nazis to clear in one go. They planned to deal with it one section at a time. The northern part was simply the first *Aktion*. The first of five, as it turned out.

Of the people living in the northern section, hundreds were shot on that first day. Thousands more were herded into the metalworking factory on Krotka Street, where many of the ghetto inhabitants usually worked. To their disgust – but not their surprise – the Jewish police and the leaders of the Jewish Council helped to herd them. Any valuable belongings the people still possessed were taken from them. The Council and the police promised that these valuables were to pay the Nazis a 'ransom' for the people's lives, meaning that they would be safe.

This was a lie. There was no ransom, no safety for any of them. All the people, including those who had given up their valuables, were taken away immediately on closed goods trains, like the one that had brought the Rosenthal family to Zbaszyn.

The Nazis told these people that they were being sent somewhere new to live. Ever hopeful, in spite of what they had been through, the people had brought suitcases and blankets and other belongings with them. But this was another lie. In truth, they were going to a place called Treblinka. It was one of several camps that the Nazis had built solely for the purpose of killing. Hardly any of the people they sent to such camps were ever seen again.

After that first transport had gone, the streets of the emptied section were strewn with abandoned bags, prams, bundles of bedding, and dead bodies. The rest of the ghetto waited with dread for their turn. It would come very soon. The whole liquidation was intended to take no more than a fortnight.

Most people simply sat and waited and hoped and prayed. Because what else could they do? But some resisted. They hid and made plans to fight back. The

Rosenthal girls were among those people. When the *Aktion* was carried out in New Market, they hoped to escape it by sheer cunning. After surviving by their wits in the ghetto for so long, they were determined to carry on in the same way.

* * *

In the gloom of the passage outside the basement room, a circle of gaunt young faces surrounded Friedel and Gina. They were all starving, with hollowed-out cheeks and dark rings under their eyes. But they looked at the twins with eager expectation, eyes glittering in the candlelight.

'Follow us,' said Gina.

There was a grimy, long-disused door at the side of the passage. Gina opened it. In the flickering light of the candle, it revealed a staircase leading down into darkness.

Beneath the building's basement was an even deeper cellar. The staircase was long, almost as steep as a ladder. At the bottom was a large space smelling strongly of mould and a mixture of rotten fish, brine and pickling vinegar. Huge barrels stood against the walls. In the days before the ghetto, market traders used this place to store their goods – the barrels would be filled with pickled herrings or gherkins. Several of the buildings around New Market had deep cellars like this one.

'If we hide down here, the Nazis won't find us,' said Friedel. Her whispered words echoed in the dank space.

Their friends looked doubtful. One of them asked, 'How? It's hardly a secret, is it?'

'We'll hide the door somehow,' said Gina. 'Cover it with cement or plaster so they can't see it.'

Another voice spoke from the gloom: 'Then how do we get in?'

'Easy. We make a secret entrance through the floorboards in the passage.'

Their friends muttered among themselves for a moment, then one of them said, 'It stinks in here.'

'It stinks up there too,' someone else replied. 'Maybe we can clean it up.'

'Exactly!' said Gina. 'We can be safe down here – I know we can.'

'We can scavenge for supplies,' Friedel added excitedly. 'There are whole streets now with nobody living in them. There must be food and stuff left behind.'

The last doubts gave way, and it was agreed. There wasn't a moment to lose. The next *Aktion* could begin any day, and they had a lot of work to do to make the cellar habitable.

They divided the work up among themselves. While some took on the disgusting job of clearing out the rotten produce from the barrels, others worked at prising up the floorboards in the passageway in front of the door. Concealing the door itself was a big challenge. A bag of cement mix was found, and a couple of the boys set about plastering over the door with a thick layer of it.

Looking at the result, everyone's heart sank. 'It sticks out like a sore thumb,' said Friedel.

It was true. The door was covered up, but the freshness of the cement was painfully obvious. If the police searched the building – which they would certainly do – they would take one look at this and guess what had been done.

'We need to dry it,' said one of the boys. 'Make it look ... well, not so new.'

Miraculously, two electric heaters were found, and even more miraculously, the electricity was on. The heaters worked, but not very well, giving out a feeble warmth. They were placed in front of the doorway and switched on. Friedel, Gina and their friends took turns sitting through the night, keeping watch on the drying. It was frustratingly slow. The electricity in the ghetto was unreliable, often cutting out, and the cement just refused to dry out properly. There were dark, damp patches all over it. But they were patient, and after another night it finally dried all over.

The doorway now looked like no more than a recess in the wall. It wouldn't stand up to close examination, but in the dim light the police probably wouldn't notice anything odd. And hopefully they wouldn't spot the loose floorboards in front of it.

Now came the task of moving everyone from the basement room down to the deep cellar. Friedel and Gina and their friends got their families ready, and they began making their way to the passage, carrying what meagre belongings they had left. The floorboards had been lifted in readiness.

It was difficult to get down, especially for the older, less agile folk. The gap was narrow because of the beams supporting the floorboards. And because it was in front of the door, it didn't lead straight on to the ladder-like staircase. You had to swing across to the stairs or just drop to the hard cellar floor. One by one the people went through. With a grunt, a prayer, or a cry of terror, they disappeared into the darkness.

Some of the older people wouldn't go. It was too difficult for them to get through, or they were frightened of the drop. One or two were terrified of the airless, reeking, deathly gloom. It seemed so deep beneath the living world.

To Friedel and Gina's dismay, one of those who were most frightened was Mum. As she followed the girls along the passage, she became more and more nervous. When they reached the hole in the floor, she froze, shaking.

'Come on, Mum,' said Gina. 'It's easier than it looks, I promise.'

Mum shook her head. Her face was pale with fright. 'I . . . I can't,' she whispered.

Friedel felt herself tensing up. She and Gina had planned this so carefully, and been so clever in thinking of it. And everyone had worked so hard to make it real. How could Mum just refuse like this? Didn't she understand the danger?

Mum looked at her daughters. She saw the pleading in their eyes, saw the love they felt for her, and their desperate need to keep her safe. And then she looked again at the deep, black, foul-smelling hole in the floor. She tensed her muscles, forcing herself to step towards it. Fear seemed to pour out of the black void – a deep, inexplicable terror that clutched at her heart and wrung it like a sponge.

'No,' she muttered. 'I'm sorry. I can't do it. I just can't go in there.'

'It's all right,' said Gina softly, and hugged her. 'You don't have to.'

Over Mum's shoulder, Gina's eyes met Friedel's. They were filled with worry and fear. What on earth were they going to do now?

* * *

The very next morning, they again heard the dreadful noise of terrified people being rounded up. This time, it was coming from right outside.

Peeping through the window, the sisters saw Nazi and Polish police marching a huge crowd of ghetto dwellers into New Market. There were thousands of them, pouring in along the streets, herded at gunpoint. To the girls' horror, they began driving some of them across the square, towards this very building.

It seemed inexplicable at first. Then it became clear. Behind the building was a large courtyard, enclosed on the other side by the rear of the buildings in the next street. It was a perfect trap. The people were forced into the courtyard and the gates were closed. Today's *Aktion* had scooped up more people than the police could deal with. This group – numbering hundreds of women, men and children – were being held in the courtyard while the rest were dealt with outside.

In the main square, the Nazis began the process they called 'selection'. This was part of every *Aktion*. The selection decided your fate – would you be kept here to work, or sent away to Treblinka? Dozens of police, armed with rifles, surrounded the Jews and made them line up in orderly groups. Many of them held little red booklets in their hands. These were the identity cards given to skilled workers in the ghetto. Most had been employed in the metal factory, and they hoped the red booklets would save their lives, by proving that they were needed for their skills.

A Nazi officer appeared. Watching through the basement window, Friedel and Gina's hearts froze. This officer was known and feared by everyone in the ghetto. Indeed, every soul living in Czestochowa was afraid of him. Captain Paul Degenhardt, the notoriously brutal chief of the Czestochowa police.

Degenhardt was a thickset man. He strode along with a swagger, swishing a riding crop. In any other circumstances, with his round face and bulbous, creased chin, he might have looked a comical figure. That was until you looked in his eyes and saw the cold, deadly light there.

As he walked along the lines, Captain Degenhardt began dividing the people into two groups, sending them to stand separately. He raised his riding crop to point at each person he passed, flicking it either to the left or the right. If he flicked it to the right, it meant the person looked strong and fit to work, and they had to go and join that group. If he flicked it to the left, it meant they looked too old or too unhealthy. After years of ghetto life, not many were healthy enough to be sent to the right.

The former factory workers held out their red booklets towards him, as if to prove that they deserved to live. He ignored them. 'You, go to the left!' he barked again and again. Eventually the market cobblestones were littered with the discarded, trampled booklets.

Those sent to the left were taken to the train station and sent away to Treblinka. What happened to them there was not known. But everyone had heard the rumours, and they were beginning to believe them.

The selection dragged on for hours, through the afternoon and beyond. The group shut inside the courtyard were put through it as well. At last, evening gloom filled New Market and silence returned. It was an uneasy, deathly silence, haunted by the events that had taken place.

When everything had grown still and it seemed safe, Friedel, Gina and Mum ventured outside. They went into the courtyard. It was littered with bits and pieces of people's discarded belongings.

While Friedel and Gina looked around, Mum wandered away towards the far end of the courtyard. When they caught up with her, she was standing in a dark corner beside an abandoned pram. Her shoulders were shaking, weeping silently.

She was a loving mother by instinct, and with only Friedel and Gina at her side she missed all her other children dreadfully, longing to have them around her again. She took to holding Leni, the doll with blonde hair that Martha had left with them, as if she were a substitute for all the real children who were gone. Mum had also begun wearing a suit jacket that had belonged to Bernard. Despite the horrifying stories they heard about what happened to people in the camps, Mum still believed that she would see him again. Max was safe in England, along with Martha. Bernard might well be alive too.

Meanwhile, the liquidation of the Czestochowa ghetto went on, relentlessly, mercilessly. Having rounded up and processed all the inhabitants of other parts of the ghetto, the Nazis turned their eyes to the buildings around New Market.

* * *

For a few days beforehand, the police drove around the area, calling out through a megaphone: 'Jews of Czestochowa, do not be alarmed. Be assured that your friends who have been sent away are happy and well in their new home.'

The van rolled along the deserted street, repeating the message. 'On the day of the next *Aktion*, you are to assemble in New Market at the appointed time. Each person who comes out voluntarily will receive a kilo of bread, a bowl of soup, some marmalade and a bar of soap. Be assured that you are perfectly safe.'

Many people wanted to believe that this was the truth. They longed to believe that the loved ones who had been taken away were alive and well.

The *Aktion* fell on a Sunday. Once again the Nazis had chosen a Jewish holy day – Simchat Torah, which celebrates the Jewish scriptures.

In the buildings around New Market itself and in nearby streets, people gathered their few treasured belongings, left their cramped, dingy rooms, and began making their way into the market square. Eventually, thousands of them had gathered there.

The people who had remained in the upper basement with the Rosenthals (those like Mum who'd refused to go into the deep cellar) got ready to go out too. Again Friedel and Gina tried to persuade Mum to go with them into the cellar and hide, but she shook her head. She wanted to, but she just couldn't do it.

'My darling daughters, you will be safe,' she said. 'I just know it. I'm old, but you're young and healthy.' Although Mum was only fifty-two years old, her suffering had aged her and damaged her health. 'The Nazis will give you work,' she said. 'You will live; you will survive.'

Friedel felt a rage boiling up inside her. Rage at the Nazis; rage at the unfairness, the cruelty, the injustice. Above all, rage at the world that had let it all happen. She suddenly picked up a wooden chair and, letting out a furious yell, brought it down with a splintering crash on the table. She smashed it down again and again, until the legs broke off and scattered over the floor. But her fury wasn't satisfied. Seizing up another chair, she did the same again. Mum and Gina watched, dumbstruck, as Friedel broke up what remained of their tatty, battered furniture.

Crying with anger, she snatched up their bedding and began to tear it to shreds.

When the rage had burned itself out, Friedel slumped down, exhausted, shoulders heaving.

There was nothing more any of them could do. Hiding was impossible. Resistance was out of the question.

'Mum, listen,' said Gina. 'If you won't hide, let's at least try and make you look healthier.'

Gina found some scraps of leftover makeup and rouged (reddened) Mum's cheeks and lips. Then she and Friedel tidied up her hair.

'There,' said Gina, trying hard to be optimistic. 'You look as young as we do.'

Outside, the loudhailer blared: 'This is the final call. Anyone not already assembled, come out now to receive your rations and ensure your safety.'

Silently, as if in a trance, Friedel, Gina and Mum stood up. Leaving the basement room, they went up the stairs, out through the front door and into the market square.

It was teeming with people – the last remaining inhabitants of the ghetto. The Nazi police went among them, beating them, insulting them, ordering them to line up. Most were women. By now all the younger men had been sent away like Bernard. They stood in a ragged line, snaking across the huge square. Some waited silently, but some were sobbing in fear and despair. Some were praying.

Captain Degenhardt, the police chief, strutted along the line, staring at each of them in turn, swishing his riding crop. The briefest look was all it took to decide a person's fate.

'You, go to the left,' he barked, and pointed with his crop. 'You to the right,' he said to the next woman. On and on, a swish of the crop, a quick scrutiny of each person's face and body, summing up the state of their health in a glance. 'You, left. And you, to the left . . . Right . . . left . . . left . . . left . . .'

From time to time there were hold-ups. Some key workers tried arguing their case, claiming that they should be spared. The police chief listened to them, sometimes annoyed, sometimes with amusement. Most of the pleas were rejected.

The selection went on for hours. Friedel and Gina had placed Mum in between them, hoping she wouldn't be singled out. Many of their younger friends were nearby, so she might just blend in. Friedel felt a glimmer of hope. As Degenhardt moved down the line towards them, there were a lot of younger people, and the number being sent to the left had grown less. Friedel reckoned about two out of every three women were being passed as fit for work and sent to the right. Mum, still wearing Bernard's old suit jacket, stood clutching Leni, silently praying. Gina moved closer to her as if to protect her. Friedel held her hand.

Degenhardt came along the line, closer and closer. Following him were two policemen armed with

truncheons. The crop flicked out and pointed at the young woman next to Gina. 'Right,' he said, and the woman turned away towards the mass of people on that side.

He moved on a step and stared at Gina with his cold, hard eyes. There was no spark of humanity or sympathy in them. She might as well have been a piece of lifeless meat on a shop counter. The crop flicked. 'Go to the right,' he said.

The cold eyes moved on to Mum, then looked at Friedel. He prodded Friedel with the end of the crop and said, 'Go right.' Looking again at Mum, after the briefest of glances he tapped her with the crop and said, 'Left.'

Gina and Friedel felt as if their hearts would seize up and stop beating. They both grabbed Mum by the arms to hold her back. In desperation they tried to pull her with them towards the right. The two policemen lashed out at them with their truncheons, grabbing hold of Mum and dragging her away from them. The truncheons slammed down on the girls' shoulders and heads, and Mum was torn from their grasp.

Friedel screamed, 'Let her go, you dirty Nazi bastards!'

'Mum, come back!' Gina wailed. 'Let her go!'

Degenhardt swore in anger, and the policemen shoved the girls away.

Mum was force-marched towards the mass of people on the left. 'Save yourselves, my babies!' she cried out to them. She was still holding Leni in one hand, and in the other a small, battered suitcase containing what remained of her belongings. 'You're still young,' she called out. 'You'll survive!'

Then she was swallowed up in the crowd. The policemen shoved Friedel and Gina brutally away towards the people on the right. Degenhardt straightened his uniform, swished his crop and carried on.

* * *

When it was all over, a fleet of heavy trucks drove into the square. All the people sent to the left that day were loaded into them. They were taken to the station, put into trains and transported to the camp at Treblinka. With that day's *Aktion*, the liquidation was complete.

Most of the tens of thousands of people who had been living in the ghetto went to Treblinka. Hardly any of them were ever seen again. Among them went most of the members of the Jewish Council and many of the Jewish police, along with their families. Betraying their people had kept them safe in the ghetto for a little while – a few months, a year or two – but in the end it had not saved them.

CHAPTER THIRTEEN

Don't Think. Don't Imagine.

That evening, silence fell over the Czestochowa ghetto. The stillness was broken from time to time by police patrols searching the buildings, looking for any Jews still hiding. But after a while they finished their business and departed. The streets were abandoned. All the windows and doorways were blank and lifeless, looking in on empty rooms.

Dazed and numbed by what they'd seen and felt that day, Friedel and Gina were herded with the other survivors to the upper end of the ghetto, to Krotka Street, where the old metal factory stood. Ghetto dwellers had worked here, but now it was used only as a place to imprison the survivors while a permanent place could be arranged for them. There were around five thousand of them. That was about a tenth of the number of people who had lived in the ghetto before the liquidation.

The twins sat together on the factory floor. They could only think of Mum. Their minds were filled with their last sight of her, disappearing into the crowd.

'They'll send them to a work camp, won't they?' said Gina. 'Mum will be all right... Won't she?' She was trying to sound optimistic, but there was doubt in her voice.

Friedel squeezed her hand. 'Of course,' she said. 'Just a work camp.'

The thought made their grief lessen a little, but they knew in their hearts that, like everything the Nazis said, it was a lie.

'I'm hungry,' said Gina, as if the feeling had taken her by surprise.

'Me too.'

The police hadn't given the people in the factory anything at all to eat. Friedel huddled down in her winter coat. With the hot summer they'd just had, she hadn't worn it for quite a while. Now the weather was growing cold, and the chill inside the old factory was creeping into her bones. She pushed her hands into the pockets and felt something hard brush against her fingers. She pulled out a small, brightly coloured cardboard box. A faint sugary aroma floated into her nostrils. Custard powder!

'Where on earth did you get that?' said Gina.

'I don't know.' Friedel frowned at it. She guessed it was a piece of grocery loot that she'd forgotten to give to their parents. It must have lain in her pocket all through the summer.

Various household bits and pieces had been discarded around the place by people who'd been sent away. Finding a saucepan and some water, they heated it over a candle flame and made themselves a big helping of custard. It wasn't much of a meal, but it helped. And it was deliciously sweet. It gave them comfort, like a sugary hug.

Along with all the other survivors, Friedel and Gina were held in the old metal factory for a long time. It all became a blur. They lost count of the days, which grew into weeks.

Then, one day at the end of October, the factory doors opened and men in uniforms ordered everyone to come outside.

These were not the Polish police. Their uniforms were different and they spoke another language. Not Polish, not German. It sounded like Russian, but it wasn't. These men were police from Ukraine, recruited by the Nazis after the invasion of the Soviet Union. Ukraine had been a part of the empire of the Soviet Union, ruled over by Russia. A great many Ukrainians volunteered to serve the Nazis, seeing them as allies against the Russians.

The Ukrainian police were supervised by men from the Gestapo – the SS special police. The SS were responsible for Nazi Germany's security. They had begun as Hitler's personal bodyguard force ('SS' stood for *Schutzstaffel*, meaning *protection squad*.) Since he came to power, the SS had grown to a colossal size, and ran all the police forces and the concentration camps. The SS even provided elite army units, who fought much more savagely and cruelly than ordinary soldiers. The Gestapo were the special police force of the SS. Their job was to root out and destroy any attempts to resist or defy the Nazis. They wore no uniforms, but they could often be spotted by their smart clothing and their attitude, as well as by the tiny Nazi badges worn on their lapels. As powerful as lords and as cruel as the devil, the Gestapo were feared by *everyone*. Even other Nazis were scared of them.

From the metal factory the people were marched along Krotka Street and into Warsaw Market, the small marketplace in the north corner of the ghetto. Across one side of the marketplace a high barbed wire fence had been erected, blocking off the entrances to three streets. There was a gate in the middle of the fence, and the people were taken through it.

They were now in the new ghetto, or the 'small ghetto' as it would become known. It consisted of a tiny corner of the old ghetto, containing just three narrow, short, dirty streets, and the whole lot was enclosed by the barbed wire fence. The only entrance was the one they had come through – the gate that opened into Warsaw Market.

These streets had long been among the poorest in Czestochowa. The buildings had already been in a bad state even before the old ghetto was created. Now the apartment blocks were filthy slums. The windows were either broken or grey with grime. Doors hung off broken hinges or had been ripped out and lay in the street. Much of the damage had been done by the police during the liquidation.

Like everywhere else, the streets and the rooms inside the buildings were littered with the remnants left behind after the liquidation. Battered and broken furniture. A single shoe lying in the gutter. Shattered bottles and crockery. A child's pushchair with a missing wheel. Heaps of rags and old clothes. A burst pillow, its feathers blowing across the pavement.

Some of the survivors who'd been held in the metal factory had lived in these streets before the liquidation. As they wandered about in a daze, occasionally someone would recognise an object that had belonged to a person they knew – a shoe, a hat, a little painted chair – and would break down crying.

Friedel and Gina walked around, trying to get their bearings. Whichever direction they turned, they could only go a short way before being blocked by the barbed wire fence.

In this tiny area, over six thousand people were now forced to find places to sleep. It was not a home, just somewhere to exist, to stay alive. Friedel and Gina found themselves living in yet another room crowded with people, most of them complete strangers.

From now on, they had only each other to live for.

* * *

Staying alive in order to work, and working in order to stay alive. That was all there was for the Czestochowa Jews now. Sleep and work. Work and sleep. And try not to die.

The Germans had a new factory in Czestochowa. A great complex of stone and steel, smoke and cinders, toxic fumes and hellish din, scarring the land like an unhealed wound.

This factory was owned by a German company called Hasag. The company worked for the Nazis, helping to supply equipment for the war. It had many similar factories across Germany and Poland, making bullets, weapons and all manner of things intended to hurt and kill. Like many other German companies under the Nazis, Hasag used forced labour – concentration camp prisoners who were forced to work for no pay in terrible conditions.

Hasag's factory in Czestochowa began operating at the same time as the big ghetto was being liquidated. Most of the survivors of the liquidation, now living in the small ghetto, were destined to work there.

* * *

1943

Friedel's eyes opened into darkness. It was four thirty in the morning. Her body ached from the cold that had seeped into her during the night.

There was a space beside her on the straw mattress, where Gina should have slept. Gina wasn't here. At this hour, she would still be at work at the Hasag factory. If she'd been here, the twins would have been able to huddle together to keep one another warm.

The factory's workers were on two shifts – day and night. The day shift worked from seven in the morning until seven in the evening. Then came the night shift. Seven until seven, seven until seven, day and night. This week Gina was on the night shift; next week it would be Friedel's turn.

Over two months had passed since the liquidation of the old ghetto, and it was now the depth of winter. In Poland, the thermometers plummeted far below zero and stayed there.

DON'T THINK. DON'T IMAGINE.

Friedel, stiff with cold, prised herself up from the mattress. Although work didn't begin for another two and a half hours, there was a lot to get through before then. The Nazis forced a strict routine on the workers, keeping close track of every one of them. Friedel rubbed her eyes and her joints, then hobbled down the stairs. There was no getting dressed – it was a very long time since anybody here had owned nightwear. They lived and slept in their only clothes.

Snow lay in the street outside, gleaming in the moonlight. It had been trampled to frozen slush in the roadway and was banked up deeply against the walls and fences. Other people were emerging from buildings all along the street, and Friedel joined the flow towards the Warsaw Market gate. Everyone on the day shift had to assemble in the square by 5 a.m. for roll call. Nobody delayed if they could help it. Any day shift worker caught inside the ghetto during working hours was likely to be shot by the SS. Only night workers and people whose jobs were inside the ghetto had permission to be there in daytime. They were given permit cards, which they guarded like precious jewels.

Hundreds of day workers lined up in the square, shivering in the cold. A loose circle of armed guards surrounded them. One by one the workers were checked off. Breakfast was doled out. There was no food, just 1 litre of lukewarm coffee per person. This was the cheap kind the Germans called *ersatz** coffee, which was made from acorns instead of coffee beans. It wasn't as nasty as you might think, and had a sweet flavour. It was all the workers had to keep them going until lunchtime.

By six o'clock, still in darkness, the workers were ready to go off to the factory. The armed Nazi guards escorted them the whole way to make sure nobody tried to make a run for freedom.

They passed through the streets that had been part of the big ghetto. Friedel's heart would grow as frozen as the snow, especially when they passed through New Market. It felt haunted. From there they marched on to the great tree-lined avenue, which Friedel had first seen in the days before the ghetto. She'd felt like a prisoner back then, when she was merely a refugee. How innocent she and Gina had been in those days.

From the avenue the marching column turned left, down the main road leading to the southern edge of the city. They could smell the factory's chemical reek before they saw it. Soon they were in through the gates and among the sprawling warren of grimy buildings.

As they arrived, the night shift workers were leaving, heading back to the ghetto with another unit of guards carrying rifles. Gina would be among them, but it was

---

* *Ersatz* means 'substitute'.

too dark and the mass of people too large for Friedel to pick her out.

The main block of the factory was a two-storey building of stone and brick, stretching out along the roadside, filled with workshops and huge factory floors. Inside here, Friedel and her workmates would labour all day.

Friedel's job was to help make the cartridge casings for rifle bullets. Great pounding machines turned sheets of brass into little shiny cylinders. As the machine went round, it churned out the casings, sending them cascading out into a big tray. The workers had to pick them out and test that they were exactly the right size and didn't have any faults.

How many of these casings would end up sending out a bullet to kill a person? Each bullet had a life-cycle. Inserted tightly into this gleaming brass case on top of a bed of explosive powder. Then into a soldier's rifle, and with a squeeze of the trigger the powder explodes, sending the bullet speeding through the air. And then ... As you held a casing in your fingers, you might picture the person who could end up in the bullet's path. A Russian soldier, maybe, or British or American. Or perhaps it would find a place in the ammunition pouch of an SS trooper or a Ukrainian policeman. The person the bullet was launched at might be a Jewish captive, just like you.

It was best not to think of it. Just keep your head bowed and work. Don't think. Don't imagine. Just work. Just stay alive.

And so the hours passed. At lunchtime each worker was given half a litre of thin soup and a chunk of bread. Then six more hours of work, while evening brought the darkness once again.

* * *

When Gina and the other night workers reached Warsaw Market, winter dawn was beginning to break over Czestochowa.

After the roll call was over, Gina made her way cautiously across the icy slush, through the gate and back into the ghetto. She was too tired even to think. Going along Nadrzeczna* Street, which was the longest of the ghetto's three streets, she found herself walking alongside a group of other young women and men. Among their faces, pinched up against the cold, she recognised two who were very familiar.

Her heart gave a little nervous jolt. She knew these men well. They were members of a secret group who called themselves Nadrzeczna 66, after the address they all lived at. They were a resistance group. They'd got together with the aim of overthrowing the Nazi tyrants. In all there were over twenty men and women in Nadrzeczna 66, and both Gina and Friedel were in

---

* This is pronounced as *Nadr–zechna*.

awe of these people's bravery. They had been smuggling guns into the ghetto, to be used whenever the day of rebellion might come. Not everyone shared the twins' admiration. Some of the ghetto's inhabitants even hated the resistance, believing that they would provoke the Nazis into wiping everyone out. They were certainly dangerous people to know.

One of the young men noticed Gina. 'How are you this lovely morning, Gina?' he said with a faint smile.

'Hi, Mendel. Not so bad. Exhausted, starving, the usual.' She smiled at the other man. 'Hi, Izidor. Tough shift? You look ready to keel over.'

Izidor shook his head. 'They won't beat me,' he said. 'We'll win through. Freedom is on the way!'

As they reached number 66, Mendel and Izidor said goodbye and went inside. Gina wondered how many weapons they had hidden inside that squat, ugly building. How many guns, how many bullets, how many Nazis might they kill? Every minute of every day they were risking their lives, smuggling and hiding such deadly secrets.

It was a little after nine o'clock when Gina got to the room in which she and Friedel had their small corner of living space. She slumped down on the straw mattress. Settling into the indent left by her sister, she was soon fast asleep.

* * *

Gina had no idea how long she'd been sleeping when she was woken by the noise of shouting and boots clattering on the stairs. Minutes, perhaps? Hours? Seconds?

'What is it?' she asked a woman who was heading for the door.

'Everyone out on the marketplace,' the woman said. She looked scared.

Another woman, looking equally terrified, added, 'They say there's going to be a selection. For Treblinka.'

Their fear went straight to Gina's heart and took root there. She hauled herself up off the mattress and joined the flood of people hurrying down the stairs. They were afraid of what waited for them in the square, but they knew that anyone caught inside the ghetto would be shot.

Hurrying along the street, Gina saw Mendel and Izidor coming out of number 66. They were deep in conversation.

'It's time,' Mendel was saying. 'We're the only ones. It's time to make a stand.'

Gina could guess what that meant. Time to fight. She knew that most of the resistance group were out at work on the day shift, either at Hasag or other workplaces. That meant that Mendel was the only resistance commander in the ghetto at this moment, and it was up to him alone whether they should resist the selection or not.

Gina hurried on towards the gate. As she walked, wherever she passed a side street she glanced towards the fence at the end of it. Polish and Ukrainian police stood just outside, guarding against anyone trying to escape.

It was around ten o'clock in the morning when Gina passed through the gate into Warsaw Market. Most of the Jews who'd been in the ghetto were already lined up. About five hundred of them in all. The selection had already begun. Gina joined the assembly alongside a group of women who worked in the same part of the Hasag factory as her.

Captain Degenhardt no longer took part in selections – at least, not in winter weather. Instead, two junior SS officers were in charge: Lieutenant Rohn and Lieutenant Schappert. Both were notoriously brutal. While armed guards surrounded the square, the two lieutenants walked along the lines of Jews. Every few steps, Rohn would stop and ask questions.

'You,' he said to one man. 'What do you do?'

'I'm a craftsman,' said the man. 'All my comrades here are craftsmen.'

Rohn glared at him and gestured to the guards. 'Take these layabouts away. To the left with them.'

The man summoned up his courage. 'Lieutenant, sir, there are no layabouts in my group. We're all first-rate craftsmen.'

Rohn glared at him. 'Very well. In that case, just *you* will go.'

If Rohn was expecting the man to grovel and plead for his life, he was disappointed. 'Yes, sir,' said the man.

Rohn was so startled, he just moved on down the line and left the craftsman alone. The man's courage, it seemed, had saved his life. Instead Rohn took out his annoyance on the next group of workers he came to. He began pulling people out of the line and shoving them towards the crowd who'd been sent to the left. Most of them were older people who had somehow survived the liquidation of the old ghetto. Some were just people that Rohn and Schappert didn't like the look of.

It was at this moment that Mendel and Izidor came out of the gate and joined a group of other young people standing in the assembly. Lieutenant Rohn noticed them. His eyes narrowed angrily. He strode towards them.

'You!' he bellowed. 'To the left! Guards, take this lot to join the others.'

What happened next was so unexpected that everyone who witnessed it remembered it a little differently. But they all remembered two things clearly. The pistol that Mendel conjured from inside his jacket and the glittering knife that suddenly appeared in Izidor's hand.

'No!' Izidor shouted. 'You can't go on killing us like this and go unpunished! You can't!'

Lieutenant Rohn just stared in astonishment. He seemed paralysed by shock. Mendel aimed the pistol at him and pulled the trigger. The crack of a gunshot echoed around the square. It hit Rohn's hand, flinging out a spatter of blood. Mendel steadied himself to take better aim, pulled the trigger, and ... nothing. The pistol just clicked. He pulled it again. *Click*.

It was as if time slowed down. While Rohn stood frozen, dripping blood, Lieutenant Schappert started to move towards Mendel, reaching out to grab him. Mendel was frantically trying to make the pistol work, shaking it and smacking it. As Schappert reached for Mendel, Izidor lunged at the SS man with his knife, jamming the point into Schappert's outstretched right arm. Schappert screamed and clutched at the wound. Mendel couldn't make the pistol work, so he turned it round in his hand and started lashing at Rohn's head with it.

At that moment, the Nazi guards recovered from their shock. A burst of gunfire echoed in the square, a ragged volley of rifle shots. Mendel and Izidor had no chance to even try to escape – they fell dead where they stood.

The guards ordered everyone in the square to put their hands up and stand motionless. Lieutenant Rohn was helped to leave, his wound dripping blood in the snow. The guards were both furious at the rebellions and elated by the opportunity to dish out punishment. They stormed in among the people, lashing out with their rifle butts.

One of them came near Gina. When she didn't move quickly enough, he raised his rifle and thrust the butt of it at her head. It landed with a sickening crack that shot pain through her whole body. Dizziness seized her and she felt herself sinking down. Then everything turned to black.

* * *

Friedel's shift finished at seven o'clock that evening. As the workers filed outside, they were a little surprised to find that the night people hadn't arrived for their shift. It was unsettling. The Nazi routine never changed. If the night shift hadn't turned up, then something serious must have happened.

The long march back to the ghetto was tense. At last they reached Warsaw Market. With their guards keeping a closer watch on them than usual, they went through roll call, then filed in through the gate.

Friedel learned quickly what had happened. It was all anyone could talk about. After the outbreak of violence, the Nazis had kept everyone standing in the square with their hands up for hours. Someone then reported the incident to Captain Degenhardt's office. As soon as he heard, he sent out a squad of SS and Gestapo to make the Jews pay for what had happened. When they arrived in the square, the SS picked twenty-five young men from the lines, at random, and shot them. Then they surrounded over five hundred people who had failed the selection and marched them away.

Eventually, after hours of standing with their hands raised, the survivors had been allowed back into the ghetto.

'But my sister,' said Friedel to someone she knew from the night shift. 'Did anyone see what happened to her?'

Nobody had seen or heard anything of Gina. Heart racing, Friedel ran to the house where they lived. She wasn't there. Their little space in the room was empty, apart from the straw mattress and their handful of belongings.

A few people were sitting around the room. 'Has anyone seen Gina?' she asked them. 'My sister. She was on the night shift.'

'I heard she was attacked by a Nazi,' said a woman who worked with Gina. 'But I didn't see it.'

'I think I saw her lying in the snow,' said another woman.

Friedel's stomach turned. 'She's dead?'

The woman shook her head sadly. 'I don't know. I'm not sure. Maybe.'

Friedel went back down to the street. Desperately she begged every person she passed – had they seen Gina?

'Yes, I saw her,' said a man from the night shift. 'I think she got hit on the head. Your friend Franka was with her.'

Franka was a Polish Jewish girl, and a close friend of both Friedel and Gina. Most of their friends these days were Polish. After the bewilderment of their first weeks in Czestochowa, the twins had learned to speak the language, Gina with ease, Friedel with more difficulty.

Friedel ran, slipping and sliding on the ice, straight for the house where Franka lived. Clattering up the rickety staircase, she burst into the room.

And there was Gina! Sitting on Franka's mattress, she was leaning back against the wall. Her eyes were half closed, her head caked in dried blood. There was a big purple bruise round the cut.

'Gina!' Friedel rushed to her. 'You're hurt. Let me look at it.'

'Oh, don't fuss, Friedel,' said Gina. Her voice was slurred.

Friedel looked at the wound carefully. 'It's going to get infected,' she said. 'It needs treatment.'

In the ghetto it was impossible to keep clean. There was no soap, no way to do laundry or wash your hair. Everyone's clothes and hair had lice in them, which could spread disease. A wound could easily become dangerously infected.

Friedel turned to Franka. 'It looks bad,' she said softly so that Gina wouldn't hear. 'We need to do something to treat it. Your dad works in the kitchen, doesn't he? Please, be a darling and run and get me some flour.'

In those days, many people who didn't have proper medicines used flour as a way of treating cuts and burns.* Friedel believed it would help.

While Franka hurried off to find some flour, Friedel went out into the streets. She needed to find something to make a fire with to heat water. Hardly anything grew in the ghetto, and it took a long time to gather enough bits of wood and sticks. Back in the room, she built a little fire in the grate and started to heat up a pan of water.

Friedel soaked a cloth and began cleaning Gina's wound. Gently she wiped away the crust of blood and removed any lice that came near it. By the time she had finished, Franka had come back with a tiny quantity of flour scrounged from the kitchen. Friedel sprinkled it on the wound, hoping it would help it to dry up and heal.

Eventually Gina went to sleep. Friedel watched over her for a while, but her exhaustion soon caught up with her and she dozed off by her sister's side.

The next morning, Friedel woke with a start. It was light outside, and she began to panic, thinking she had missed roll call and the start of her shift. But looking around, she saw that all the occupants of the room were still there, exactly as they'd been the night before.

---

* Doctors advise that this is *not* a helpful thing to do, especially for burns. Flour can actually make things worse. Before modern medicine, so-called 'folk remedies' were very common. Some actually worked, but most didn't.

DON'T THINK. DON'T IMAGINE.

Nobody would be going to work today. After yesterday's violent events, the ghetto was on lockdown.

Gina was soon well enough to make the short walk back to their own room. Her wound was looking better already. Despite Friedel's worries, it hadn't got infected. Not badly, anyway. Gina would have a scar, but she wasn't going to die.

After a few days, the lockdown was over and everyone went back to work. When Friedel's shift marched out to the marketplace, she noticed that the bodies were still lying where they had fallen in the snow. She gritted her teeth. There was nothing she or anyone else could do about it.

The answer was the same as always. Just keep your head bowed and walk on. Don't notice. Don't think. Don't imagine. Just work. Just stay alive. Keep on living, for yourself, for the ones you love.

CHAPTER FOURTEEN

The Camp

After its bitter winter, the Czestochowa ghetto would never see another full summer. The Nazis and the Hasag company were fed up with bringing their workers to and from the ghetto each day. From now on, they were going to make things more efficient. The workers from the ghetto would live at the factory.

In June, less than seven months after creating the small ghetto, the Nazis brought about the final liquidation. Not just a liquidation this time, but a complete and utter destruction. The people were forced out, hunted and routed out of cellars and hiding places, brutally herded to the market square. Then the Nazis set about destroying the buildings with dynamite.

Hour after hour, the ground was shaken repeatedly by huge explosions. By the time the work was finished, there was hardly a building left standing in the ghetto's three streets. Here and there the stumps of chimneys and remnants of walls stuck up from a sea of bricks and rubble.

Of course the Nazis held a selection, picking out those who were still healthy enough to work. Friedel and Gina passed. Together with the other fortunate souls, they began the march through the city to the Hasag factory. This would be the last time they would make the journey. From now on they would be living at Hasag, in the factory's very own concentration camp.

* * *

Friedel and Gina walked, side by side, surrounded by hundreds of others who'd been brought from the destroyed ghetto. The guards herded them through the Hasag complex. They passed by the workshops and the sprawling main building, then along a roadway the sisters had never seen before. Their marches to work had never taken them this far inside the complex.

Railway tracks lined the road. The main Czestochowa railway line went by the Hasag works in a great bend that hugged the edge of the river. Branch lines came off it into the factory grounds, and trains steamed in each day to deliver materials and collect finished products. The tracks went right through the grounds, so the wagons could roll up to the factory loading bays.

The prisoners were marched along the tracks to the far end of the complex. On the left of the roadway was a high barbed wire fence. A little way along, they came to a big gate. The guards barked orders and began driving the prisoners through it. Another shouted an order, and they halted at last.

Friedel and Gina looked around. They were in an open square, like a parade ground. This was what the Nazis called the *Appelplatz*, or roll-call square. It was surrounded on three sides by long, low buildings made of wood – barrack blocks for the prisoners.

This would be their home from now on. Or rather, their place of existence, where they would eat and sleep and suffer. Nothing like this could be a home, by any stretch. The Jews of Czestochowa would no longer be ghetto dwellers; they were now even lower, if that was possible. They would be Jewish prisoners in a Nazi concentration camp.

The part Friedel and Gina were in was the women's section of the camp. The men's section was on the other side of another high barbed wire fence that divided the roll-call square in two. The camp wasn't very big. There were only eight barracks in the women's section, and even fewer on the men's side.

Friedel and Gina had never seen a concentration camp before, let alone been inside one. But they'd heard the stories and rumours. They were known to be evil places, where prisoners' lives were brutal and short – worse than any ghetto.

At first sight the Hasag camp didn't look particularly impressive. Just some newly built wooden barrack buildings, fences all around, and here and there a high watchtower. It seemed bleak and miserable rather than scary. That was until you noticed the armed guards patrolling the fences and gazing out from the towers.

In fact, Hasag camps weren't quite the same as other Nazi concentration camps. The main ones – places like Auschwitz, Dachau and Buchenwald – were owned and run by the SS. Hasag camps were controlled by Hasag itself, and were guarded by the company's own private force, called the Labour Guard. Even so, these camps were just as dangerous for their prisoners, and the Labour Guard could be every bit as nasty as the SS.

The lieutenants and captains of the Labour Guard were mostly German. The ordinary guards were mainly the so-called *Volksdeutsche*, the 'German folk', who had been Polish citizens before the war but considered themselves German. They were disliked by both the Germans and the Poles. There were also Ukrainians in the Labour Guard. They were especially brutal, perhaps because only that kind of man would volunteer to serve their Nazi conquerors.

Under the guards' cold, hard gaze, Friedel and Gina and their friends lined up in the square. Their names and details were taken, and then they were shown to their barracks. The buildings were new but poorly built, like great big garden sheds, reeking of wood preserver. Inside were rows of high wooden bunks that were more like shelves than beds.

The prisoners weren't given any clothes to wear. There were none of the usual striped uniforms that were worn in concentration camps. This was another difference between Hasag camps and SS camps – the prisoners had to live and work in whatever clothes they arrived in. For the ghetto people, that often meant the very poorest clothing, the last threadbare garments they were left with after selling everything else for food. For Friedel and Gina it meant the dresses with the torn collars they'd worn at Father's funeral.

If prisoners weren't already in threadbare tatters when they arrived at the camp, the conditions inside meant they soon would be. By the time winter came, some of them would have to resort to wrapping themselves in rags, or even paper. Anything to try to keep out the dreadful cold.

The camp itself was only a small part of their existence, though. Their waking hours – which were long – continued to be spent in the hell of the factory.

* * *

Machines thrummed and rumbled, roared and shrieked. The din filled the huge halls, echoing off the high roof, and the place reeked of metal and oil. The floor and the very air vibrated.

In the inspection department, Friedel sat at a conveyor belt on which the brass bullet casings passed by, gleaming under the dazzling lights. Her hands darted quickly back and forth, picking casings off the conveyor, checking them, measuring them and carefully placing them on a large tray beside her. Once the tray was full, it would be taken to the next section of the factory to be stamped and have the bullets inserted. Every now and then, she would find a casing that had been squashed a bit out of shape or scratched by the machinery. She would pick it out and throw it into the scrap basket. From there it would be fed back into the system for recycling.

To Friedel's left and right, other women and girls were doing the same work, all moving as fast as she was. If you didn't do enough casings every hour, you would be in trouble. A beating was the usual punishment. The little shiny objects spun through their fingers and lined up quickly on the trays in glittering, tinkling rows. Having to work so fast made it easy to miss slight faults. There was punishment for that, too.

Overseeing the whole operation was the supervisor, Mr Herr. His office was up on a higher level, with windows looking out over the factory floor. Every so often he would come out and stand on the walkway, staring down at the women working below. Friedel was terrified of Mr Herr. They all were. He regularly came down and inspected their work, and it made their skin crawl with fear and loathing every time.

Friedel heard his heavy footsteps on the steel walkway, and dread clutched at her heart. He walked along the production line, checking each woman's tray of casings. Friedel's neck prickled as he passed behind her ... then flushed with relief as he moved on down the line. It wasn't just fear of punishment that made Friedel and the other girls nervous. Mr Herr had a way about him – he was creepy around the female workers.

There weren't any male prisoners working in the inspection hall. Whenever men came in on some errand, the women weren't allowed to talk to them. If they did, it could earn them a slap from Mr Herr or one of the other supervisors. Incredible as it might seem, working in the inspection hall was one of the best jobs in the factory.

Other less fortunate souls worked with toxic chemicals or dangerous heavy machinery. These poor people were often injured.

From the corner of her eye Friedel saw Mr Herr pick up another girl's casing tray. It was only a quarter full. Friedel knew what was about to happen.

'What the hell is this?' he shouted. 'You think this is some kind of holiday camp? Eh? Think you can just take it easy? Upstairs to my office, *now*!'

He grabbed the girl by the collar and force-marched her to the stairs. Friedel kept her eyes fixed on her work. The same thing had happened to her, and to many of the other women. She knew very well what was in store for the girl. The beating was only a part of it.

When it was over, the girl returned to her stool and went back to work, head bowed, trying her best to work faster.

Perhaps it was the distraction that made Friedel lose focus on her work, or perhaps it was just exhaustion, hunger, fear. But she suddenly realised that Mr Herr was standing behind her again. He leaned past her and picked a couple of casings off her tray, peering at them. Friedel's whole body tensed. Without even looking she could sense that he wasn't happy with what he saw. He checked them with a measuring gauge, breathing heavily. He was so close that she could hear the rasp of his breath above the factory noise.

With a bellow that made her nearly jump out of her skin, he shoved the casings in front of her face. 'Look at these! Do they look right to you?'

Friedel looked. One of them had a minute dent on the rim. The other one had nothing wrong with it that she could see. But she knew better than to argue. She shook her head.

'Speak up!' he roared. 'Do they look right to you?'

'No, sir.'

'They look like a dog made them! A blind bat could see they're faulty!' His voice rose even higher in his rage. 'What the hell is wrong with you animals? Why can't you check these things properly! Don't you know good German lives depend on the work you do?'

There was a stack of wooden boxes near him, filled with freshly made casings waiting to be spread on the conveyor. Red in the face, out of control, he shoved the stack over with all his strength. One of them flew at Friedel. She tried to dodge, but it clipped her ankle, gouging a deep cut.

Mr Herr stormed back to his office, leaving Friedel shaking and clutching her stool for support. Blood was running down into her shoe. She had no socks or stockings, just bare feet inside her shoes. There was nothing she could do right now – she just had to ignore the injury and get back to work.

In a concentration camp, with the terrible conditions the prisoners lived in, any injuries could threaten your life. Infections were the main danger. Another was the permanently bad state of the prisoners' health. As well as making you generally weak, poor health made infections more likely to become dangerous. By the next evening, Friedel's cut ankle still wasn't healing up. She showed it to Gina.

'Why won't it heal?' she asked.

Gina didn't know. 'Maybe the cold weather?'

Neither of them could know for sure, and there were no doctors or nurses to ask.

'Well, you know what Mum used to say,' Gina said.

'If you're in trouble, the best medicine is your own you-know-what.'

'Oh god,' muttered Friedel, and laughed. 'I remember.'

Germans have a few different words for it – *Pipi*, *Pisse*, *Natursekt* (nature's sparkling wine). Call it what you will, Mum had always been very sure of her traditional wisdom. So Friedel carefully collected some and washed the injury with it. Over the following days, miraculously, the cut finally started to heal up.*

Whether the 'sparkling wine' had really helped, who can say, but it had been a close call. If an injury like that became infected, it would certainly have been *off to the left* for Friedel at the next selection. But although the ankle improved, it still wasn't fully better when the selection took place.

Selections happened often in the Hasag camp. The work, the starvation and the diseases that prowled the barracks wore people down, even though they were young and had started out healthy. Many were sent away. Not to Treblinka any more – that evil place had been closed down. The people sent to the left were instead transported to Auschwitz, a huge concentration camp, which was also a death camp. Its very name froze the blood. Every selection was more frightening than

---

* As with using flour, doctors advise against treating injuries with urine. It isn't sterile, and can actually make things worse.

the last, because your health was always that little bit worse.

For Friedel this one was terrifying. Lining up, she couldn't stop thinking, *Will I be selected? Will I get to live another day?*

There was a blonde-haired German woman who worked for Hasag and helped supervise the selections. The prisoners nicknamed her Petrushka, which is the name of a vegetable that looks like a white carrot. Petrushka was cruel and vicious and not very bright. A large, heavily built woman, she manhandled and hurt the prisoners, and loved to see their fear and suffering as they waited to find out who went right and who went left.

As the officer came towards Friedel and looked her up and down, she saw Petrushka's mocking eyes smiling. Friedel's insides froze. The cut felt like a shrieking, flashing alarm crying out, '*Pick this one! Unhealthy! Unfit!*' The moment went on and on and ... the officer moved along. A flicker of disappointment crossed Petrushka's face, then she switched her eager gaze to the next poor soul.

Friedel was safe. For the time being. Until the next selection or the next injury or the next illness – whichever came soonest.

* * *

In the world outside, beyond Hasag, far beyond Czestochowa, big events were happening. As the year turned from 1943 to 1944, the war was going badly for Nazi Germany. They suffered defeat after defeat. Their campaign in the east against the Soviet Union had turned into an utter disaster. By the middle of 1944 it became obvious that Germany was going to lose the war. The only question was how long it would take, and how many lives it would cost.

In the west, the British, Americans, Canadians and other countries' forces – 'the Allies' as they were known – invaded Nazi-occupied France. It started on D-Day, 6 June 1944. From that moment on, the Allies began slowly pushing the Germans out of France, then out of Belgium and the Netherlands.

D-Day was a huge event for the world, but to people in Czestochowa it was a very long way away. Fragments of news trickled through, whispered from person to person, and these gave them a tiny bit of hope.

The fighting in the east was much closer to them, and therefore more important. There the Germans were fighting against the Soviet Union. Known as the 'Red Army', the Soviet forces were colossal, numbering many millions of soldiers. Both men and women fought in the front lines as infantry soldiers, tank crews and fighter pilots. Most were Russians, but there were also people from all the different parts of their empire, including Ukrainians who hadn't sided with the Nazis.

Gradually the Red Army was forcing the Germans out of the lands they had conquered. Out of Russia, out of Belarus, out of Ukraine. And now it was pushing its way into Poland.

It was a bitter war. The Nazis and the Soviets hated each other with a cruel passion, and fought without mercy. Millions of Soviet soldiers who were captured by the Germans were sent to concentration camps and died there. German soldiers taken by the Soviets could expect no better treatment.

With Germany struggling to slow down their defeat, conditions for their prisoners got worse and worse. In

the camps, it was dreadful. As 1944 went on, life in the Czestochowa Hasag camp became a daily nightmare. Whether a person survived to the end of each day was down to simple luck as much as anything. Friedel and Gina and their friends stuck close together, doing whatever they could to help each other stay alive. Shielding each other from the guards and overseers, sharing food, keeping each other warm.

With each passing week, the Red Army was coming ever closer, fighting their way across Poland, forcing the Germans to retreat. By the end of 1944, they had reached the great river Vistula. The Vistula is a blue thread that flows from the south of Poland all the way to the Baltic Sea in the north, dividing the country in half. On the river's east bank, the Red Army paused for a while. Its commanders waited through the midwinter, preparing their forces for a massive onslaught. Over 2 million soldiers, with thousands upon thousands of tanks and big guns, were lined up, all the way along the Vistula, ready to launch their attack.

Czestochowa was only 190 kilometres away.

The Soviet soldiers knew the kind of things the Nazis had been doing in their camps. In summer 1944 they had captured a number of camps around the cities of Lublin and Warsaw. One of them, called Majdanek, had shocked them deeply. It was a huge concentration camp where prisoners had been murdered in vast numbers.

They had also discovered Treblinka. Hundreds of thousands of Jews had been sent to Treblinka from the ghettos in Czestochowa, Warsaw and other cities. And yet there was little for the Soviets to find. The SS had tried to hide what had been done there. They had demolished all the camp buildings, and cleared away the rubble. They burned and destroyed nearby villages to make sure there were no witnesses, and they even ploughed the ground and sowed it with wild flowers.

But it wasn't enough. Nothing could ever be enough to completely erase what the Nazis had done at Treblinka. When Soviet soldiers walked through the place where the camp had been, they found small remnants among the ploughed soil. A bit of tattered clothing half-buried. A shoe. A shaving brush. A stained, torn passport. The traces could never be altogether removed. Each item was a witness to the evil that had been done here.

After Majdanek and Treblinka and the other camps they'd found, the Red Army advanced on, their hatred against the Nazis burning hotter than ever.

They discovered more and more camps – mostly the small outlying ones. Hundreds upon hundreds of them were scattered all across Poland. Most were empty by the time the Red Army arrived. Before the Germans retreated, they'd evacuated the camps, forcing the survivors to march west through the bitter snows of a Polish winter. They were taken to other camps, further away from the advancing Soviets.

Many prisoners died during the long treks, and so they became known as the 'Death Marches'. Week by week, as 1944 ended and 1945 began, more camps were emptied. The Death Marches became a torrent, pouring along the roads and railway lines towards Germany.

* * *

On a dark morning in the middle of January, Friedel and Gina and the other women in their barrack were woken with a shock.

The early morning wake-up was always a nasty jolt to everyone's system. Every concentration camp prisoner knew it well – the sudden, violent whistle, opening your eyes into darkness because the sun hadn't even begun to glimmer yet. On this day, the women could tell right away that something was wrong.

For weeks they'd been hearing rumours. *The Russians are on their way.* If you listened carefully, you could hear their big guns in the distance. Now the Red Army was not only close – its front-line soldiers were actually in the eastern suburbs of Czestochowa.

For the past month, the SS had been running the factory and the camp. The Hasag company had been pushed out. The Labour Guard had gone, and their place had been taken by SS concentration camp guards. Sensing that their reign of terror was in its dying days, the

SS guards' discipline was slack, and they were more cruel and violent than usual.

With the Red Army so close, the SS commanders in Czestochowa decided that the time had come to evacuate.

With the wake-up whistle still ringing in their ears, Friedel and Gina hauled themselves stiffly from their bunk. They pulled on their shoes, folded their thin, scratchy blankets neatly, and filed out of the door into the roll-call square.

It was a scene of chaos. All the workers from the night shift had been brought back to the camp and were lining up in the square. On the other side of the fence, in the men's camp, the same thing was happening.

From habit, the prisoners all began forming up into lines, ready to receive their meagre breakfast, answer the roll call, and march off to the factory. But as they waited, it became even clearer that today was not like other days.

The guards ordered the prisoners to be silent as the factory director, Mr Liht, got up on a podium and began to give a speech. The loudspeakers squealed, then his strident voice rang out.

'Workers of Hasag,' he said. 'With great reluctance, and according to the wishes of our beloved leaders, you are all to be moved. This place is no longer safe for you. The Soviet menace is close at hand. They are a danger to all Jews. We care greatly for your well-being, and intend to keep you safe.'

Friedel, Gina and all the other prisoners listened in dumbfounded disbelief. Did the Nazis actually believe they were *protecting* the Jews?

Mr Liht went on. 'Therefore you will be transferred immediately to a camp in Germany, where you will be protected from the Russian evil. Be obedient, and no harm will come to you. In your new camp you will be bathed and given new clothes, and you will be well fed and cared for.'

As soon as this astonishing speech was finished, the guards forced the prisoners back into their barracks. They were ordered to gather whatever belongings they had and be ready to go right away.

The guards surrounded all the barrack buildings. Some people managed to escape, and found hiding places in among the factory buildings. Friedel and Gina and their friends were not so lucky. Being inside the barrack when it began, they were trapped.

After a short, extremely anxious wait, the evacuation started.

They trooped out to the roll-call square once more, and from there the guards herded them out through the gate. A train stood on the tracks, hissing steam.

It wasn't unusual to see trains waiting to move into the loading docks. But this train wasn't delivering anything. It had come to collect. It was made up of typical goods wagons, with their big sliding doors standing open. To

Friedel and Gina and many of their friends, they looked horribly familiar.

The prisoners were forced into the dark, damp wagons. By the time the loading was finished, it seemed to Friedel that there must be a hundred people in the wagon, along with her and Gina. There was hardly room to stand or to sit on the floor.

With a clang the door slid shut. Darkness. They began to move.

Not a single person on the train had the slightest idea where they were going or what fate awaited them.

CHAPTER FIFTEEN

These Were Once People

1945

Gina pressed her eye to a crack between the planks of the wagon wall. She wanted to get some idea of where they were heading, but all she could see was countryside going by. They could be anywhere.

'It's only been half a day,' said Friedel. 'We won't be there yet.'

'I want to know where we're heading,' Gina replied.

'Well, can you tell?'

Gina sighed. 'No.'

Reluctantly, she stopped peering out. After staring into daylight, she was now blinded by the darkness inside the wagon. It was a heaving, stinking darkness of dozens of people packed tightly together. Friedel was sitting on the floor with her knees pulled up tight to her chest. That was the only way you could sit – there was no question of stretching out, let alone lying down.

Feeling her way back to her space next to Friedel, Gina's hand landed on something soft. She tried to pick it up, but it was big and heavy, and people were standing on part of it. Gina heaved at it. Grumbling, people shifted position and it came free. It was an eiderdown – a bed covering a bit like a duvet. In those days, people used eiderdowns as an extra covering on top of their sheets and blankets. They were filled with soft duck feathers and were expensive. Only better-off people had them.

As her eyes grew used to the dark, Gina could make out the fine embroidery covering the eiderdown. It must have once been somebody's precious possession. It would have covered a big, comfy bed in a nice house, perhaps somewhere in Germany, maybe in a city like Dusseldorf or Berlin. Or more likely some quiet town in another country, Hungary perhaps. At the foot of the bed a cheerful fire probably burned in the grate in winter, and there'd be a window looking out over fields or perhaps a town square. Gina pictured a happy home, a pleasant Jewish family like hers, who gathered round the table for Shabbos dinner. Each day the mother of the house would make the bed, carefully smoothing out the eiderdown. Maybe sometimes the kids would bounce on the bed and get told off.

Then the Nazis came. The family were ordered out of their house, made to line up. They took whatever they could carry. The mother must have grabbed the eiderdown, for comfort and warmth for the children, and for the memories it held. Carrying their bags and suitcases, they were driven into this wagon with dozens of others. Mum probably told the kids there was nothing to fear, that they were just going to a new place to live.

Where had the train taken them? Most likely Auschwitz. When they arrived, they were bundled out on to the unloading ramp. The eiderdown, too bulky to carry, was left behind, shoved into a corner of the wagon. Trampled and soiled, the precious memories of the family's life had faded.

Gina and Friedel huddled together, pulling the eiderdown round them. It was big, and they managed to get several of their friends under it too. Tightly packed, they kept each other warm through a long night.

Everyone was hungry. All they'd had to eat was a bit of bread. The prisoners had been given several round flat loaves. It was the kind called *Schwarzbrot* – black bread. Each loaf had to be divided into sixteen pieces so that each person could get some. That had been hours ago.

Another day came. Just cracks of light through the sides of the wagon. Then another and another, and still the train rumbled slowly on. It stopped often, sometimes to take on water for the steam locomotive, sometimes for no obvious reason. Nazi Germany was falling apart, and the railways were in chaos. So many people to be moved, so many soldiers retreating. The Allied air forces kept on bombing the main tracks and destroying locomotives. The Germans repaired the tracks as quickly as the bombers could wreck them, but there were constant delays.

Friedel kept a careful count of the days. She had reached eight on the day they finally arrived at their destination. They'd left the Hasag camp on 16 January, which meant that today was her and Gina's birthday. They were twenty-one years old.

The wagon door opened. It was night-time. Because of the risk of bombers, there were no lights, no torches. The women clambered out. Men in SS uniforms with rifles and fierce-looking dogs were there to guard them, shove them, push them towards the camp that would be their new prison – their new hell. Its name was Bergen-Belsen.

Friedel and Gina had seen and experienced terrible things. The street violence of the Brownshirts in Dusseldorf, Father's business being taken away, the police raiding their home in the night, the misery of Zbaszyn, the ghetto, the SS, the selections, the killings, the starvation. But even after all that, they still hadn't seen the very worst the Nazis could do. At Bergen-Belsen they saw it at last. Alongside Auschwitz, Bergen-Belsen would come to be viewed as the

very pit of Hell. Its very existence was not only the worst of Nazi crimes, but the ultimate human evil.

Inside the camp, the prisoners were marched to a building. There, they were ordered to take off all their clothes and leave them in a pile, together with any belongings. Then they had to file through to a shower room. The showers were ice cold and there were no towels.

Dripping and shivering, Friedel, Gina and the other women and girls lined up to be given their camp uniforms. Their names and details were put on the camp register. The people handing out the clothing and taking their names were prisoners, supervised by SS guards.

The uniforms were second- or third-hand. Friedel looked at hers in bewilderment and disgust. This was her first sight of the striped concentration camp uniform. It consisted of a shapeless coat, like a big sack with buttons up the front. Nothing else – no trousers or dress. The stripes had once been white and blue, but wear and grime had turned them to shades of light and dark grey. There was no underwear, no socks or stockings. A pair of battered shoes was shoved at Friedel. Gina was given a pair of wooden clogs.

They never saw their meagre belongings again. Gina's harmonica was gone forever.

Once they were dressed, the guards forced everyone out through the door. It was savagely cold January weather, and they were still dripping wet. The water quickly turned to icicles in their hair.

Friedel and Gina clung together, shuddering, terrified of what might happen to them next. All the way from Czestochowa they'd been afraid, but now the fear grew stronger. They'd never experienced anything like this.

The guards marched the women and girls to a wooden barrack building in a far corner of the camp. Inside it was completely empty. No beds or bunks, no stove for warmth. There was a washroom at one end, but nothing else. This, they were told, was their barrack block, where they would be living from now on.

Until a few days before, this building had been part of a prisoner-of-war camp for captured Soviet soldiers. It was one of a group of buildings that had been the camp's hospital. The POW camp had closed down and now its former hospital was part of the the concentration camp. It was badly needed. The main sections of the camp had become horribly overcrowded because of prisoners being transported from elsewhere. Now the emptied hospital buildings had become barracks for women prisoners.

The buildings had been cleared out, so there was nothing to sleep on. Friedel, Gina and a dozen or so of their friends found a place on the floor. The only way to avoid freezing to death was to huddle tightly together in a big heap, each body helping to warm others. Other groups did the same. Exhausted, hundreds of women and girls, cold and frightened, slept through the night in each other's arms.

* * *

After a year and a half in the Hasag camp, they weren't surprised to be woken at five o'clock the next morning.

A woman prisoner came into the barrack and ordered them outside. Friedel and Gina and their friends were astonished by the nasty, aggressive way this older prisoner acted, shoving and insulting them. This was their first experience of a concentration camp 'kapo'. A kapo was a prisoner who worked for the SS as a kind of slave-driver. Some were in charge of work gangs; others supervised barrack blocks. Many of them loved the power they'd been given and used it to bully and beat people. Most kapos were criminal prisoners, not Jews.

Stiff from the cold, hard floor, and still exhausted, the women and girls trudged out to the roll-call square. While the roll was being called, big containers of acorn coffee were brought. Each prisoner got a cup, and that was their breakfast for the day. Large bundles of straw were brought and dumped in the square, along with a stack of old blankets.

'That's for your beds,' said the kapo. 'Take it all inside.'

Friedel and Gina picked up a blanket each. They realised that all the blankets were crawling with lice, defeating the purpose of the showers. After a night under these blankets, their uniforms and bodies would be as louse-ridden as when they'd arrived from Czestochowa.

There was no work that day, so the sisters explored the camp, trying to find out what kind of place they'd been brought to.

The women's section of the camp – the part that had been a hospital – had a lot of open space. The old hospital barrack buildings were scattered about like lodges in a holiday camp. Through the fence, Friedel and Gina could see the other areas of the camp. The barrack blocks there were tightly packed together in rows. Like the Hasag camp, the male prisoners were in a separate section, cut off from the women by several fences and a road. The whole camp was surrounded by a tall electrified fence, with wooden guard towers.

Watching the prisoners move about in the other parts of the camp, the sisters were horrified to see the state they were in. The two of them had lived with hunger for several years now, but what they saw in Bergen-Belsen went beyond that. Many of the prisoners were so thin, their limbs were like sticks. Even more alarming, Friedel and Gina learned that typhus, a deadly disease, was rampant in the camp. More transports of prisoners from other camps were arriving all the time, and it was becoming desperately overcrowded. That caused the typhus to spread.

And yet still the twins had not seen the worst that Bergen-Belsen had to offer.

* * *

What a place to turn twenty-one in – to become a proper grown-up at last. Half their childhood and all of Friedel and Gina's teenage years had been stolen from them by the Nazis. The twins were determined to take something back, to recover a little glimmer of hope and love to light the darkness. Each of them decided to make the other a birthday present.

All they had were the sack-like uniforms they wore. Gina sat on her straw bed and examined hers. It was made of thick cotton, with plastic buttons. The top half and sleeves had a lining in them, made of a surprisingly soft grey material. It had a slightly satiny feel.

Gina went to her friend Franka, who knew a lot about sewing and making clothes. Franka was older, and had been trained by an underwear maker, as Martha had. Gina and Friedel hadn't worked at Mrs Boehrer's long enough to learn more than the basics.

'What do you think?' Gina asked her. 'We've got no underwear. Can I make something from this lining for Friedel?'

'Did you have anything in mind?' Franka asked, looking at the lining.

Gina said the first thing that popped into her head. 'Socks, maybe?' Her wooden clogs were too small, and she had blisters on her heels. She missed having socks, and knew Friedel did too. 'Yes, socks,' she said.

Franka thought for a moment, then spoke to one of the other girls, whose name was Ilse. Then they spoke to another friend of Gina's, called Judyta. From somewhere, Judyta conjured a needle, and Ilse a small pair of scissors.

They'd brought these precious objects all the way from Czestochowa, and had managed to keep hold of them when they arrived here.

Once Franka had helped her get started, Gina sat on her bed and cut out pieces of the lining. It made her happy to be able to do this for her twin, and she worked on the socks with intense concentration.

Meanwhile, Friedel also spoke to Franka.

'What do you want to make?' Franka asked her.

Friedel wasn't sure. 'What kind of things did you used to make, Franka?'

'I used to work on bras, mostly.'

Friedel recalled her time in Mrs Boehrer's sewing room, learning to cut and stitch alongside Martha and Gina. At the time it had seemed like bad things were happening in the world. Now, looking back, it seemed blissful and cosy. Most of the skills from those long-ago days were lost to Friedel now, but she jumped at the idea of making a bra for Gina. It would make her so happy.

'OK,' she said. 'But it's complicated. I'll need your help.'

Franka cut out the various pieces they would need from the lining of Friedel's uniform. Then, using threads pulled out from the fraying material, she helped stitch them together. It was difficult without all the usual catches and elastic, but Friedel did the best that she could.

Together they worked, the five friends. Friedel, Franka, Ilse, Judyta and Gina, aglow with the joy of making gifts out of scraps of material and oceans of love. For a few magical hours, the world outside their little circle, beyond the barrack walls, did not exist.

When the gifts were ready, Friedel and Gina exchanged them. 'Happy twenty-first!' they said, and hugged, laughing.

It was a good evening, a little fragment of joy that the twins and all their friends desperately needed. After today, there would be no more happiness in Bergen-Belsen.

* * *

On the second morning, after roll call several kapos – all as unpleasant as the first – organised the women for their work assignments. Friedel and Gina and a couple of their friends were placed together in the same group.

'Follow me,' said a sour-faced kapo. 'No straying, or you'll get the sharp end of a whip.'

They followed her through a gate, out on to the access road that ran through the middle of the camp. On the other side was another guarded gate leading into another section of the camp.

As they'd seen the day before, the barrack blocks here were tightly packed together in two rows, with a roll-call square to one side. From the kapo's grunted comments, they learned that this was the original women's section. (The men's section was further along the roadway, towards the camp's main gate.)

'In here,' said the kapo, and flung open the door of the nearest barrack block.

Puzzled, they went inside. At first sight, it looked like a typical camp block, lined with shelf-like bunks on both sides. It appeared to be empty of people. Glancing around, Friedel realised that one end was completely filled with a gigantic stack of objects piled up halfway to the ceiling. She blinked and peered again. There was a loud gasp from the other women. Somebody said, 'Oh hell, no. God have mercy.'

Friedel felt her throat tighten as if she was going to be sick. She'd been wrong – the barrack was not empty of people. It was just empty of living, breathing people.

The kapo gave a bitter little laugh at the women's shock. 'Pull yourselves together, missies. You're taking this lot to the pit.' As they stood staring, she clapped her hands impatiently. 'Well, what're you waiting for? There's barrows outside. Move!'

With difficulty, Friedel and Gina and the other women forced themselves to approach the awful heap. Their years in the ghetto and in Hasag had taught them to steel themselves. Don't think, don't imagine. Just go on living. Think of them as objects. Just objects to be moved.

Objects that just happened to have once been people and weren't any more.

One by one, the women helped each other carry the objects out of the barrack. They placed them in large wooden wheelbarrows. Then, in teams, they hauled the heavy barrows across the square to a big fenced-off area at the corner of the camp. Huge, deep pits had been dug. While the kapo barked orders and insults at them, the women had to unload the objects and lay them in the nearest pit. It was already half-full.

'Typhus did this,' said the kapo, and gave another of her mirthless chuckles. 'Watch you don't catch it, or you'll be on the barrow too!'

As she worked, Friedel felt herself changing. Object after object was carried out from the barrack to the barrow and then laid in the pit. *Who were you?* she couldn't stop herself thinking. *Who did you belong to? Who loved you?* And with each of them, it was as if a door closed somewhere inside her. A part of herself, a part of her heart, her soul, was shut off. Another object, another door snapping closed. She grew more and more numb. But the rooms in her mind that were closed off did not lie empty. Inside was locked a sorrow. A sorrow so deep that, behind those doors, silently, for as long as she lived, a part of her would never stop weeping.

How could this happen? she asked herself. *Why did it happen? How was it allowed to happen?* No answers came. It was beyond understanding.

* * *

Day after day the dreadful work went on. Meanwhile, the camp became ever more overcrowded. From all directions the Allied armies were forcing the Germans to retreat. More concentration camps were being evacuated, and thousands of prisoners were transferred to camps that were nearer to the centre of Germany. With Bergen-Belsen becoming full to bursting, the typhus epidemic ran out of control.

Mercifully, Friedel and Gina didn't catch the disease. Even more mercifully, their time in Bergen-Belsen was cut short. They'd only been there for three weeks when an announcement was made at roll call. The SS were asking for volunteers to work in an aeroplane factory.

Both Friedel's and Gina's hands shot up. All their friends did the same. So did several hundred of the other women who'd come with them from Czestochowa. They all knew how terrible it could be to work in a Nazi factory, but it could never be worse than here.

The volunteers' names were taken, and that was that. They were sent back to their usual work assignments.

A couple of days later at roll call, the officer in charge read out a list. His voice came piercingly through the squealing loudspeakers:

'The following prisoners are to be transferred to the labour detail for the Kuno I aircraft factory.'

He began reading the list. Dozens of names were reeled off. Friedel and Gina and their friends waited anxiously. This would be their one and only chance to get away from this vile, terrifying place.

The list was in alphabetical order, so it would take time to get to Rosenthal. Franka's name was called. She gave a little yelp of relief. So did Ilse and Judyta when their names were read out. Several other friends were also on the list. At last the officer got to the *R* names. Gina clutched Friedel's hand in hers.

'Regina Rosenthal,' squealed the loudspeaker.

Gina breathed, '*Yes*.' Her eyes met Friedel's and they smiled nervously as they waited to hear the next name.

The loudspeaker barked, 'Gilda Rubenstein.' Then another name, then another and another.

Friedel let out a gasp of dismay. It couldn't be. It was impossible. They couldn't be separated, not now! Not after all they'd been through! More names went by. Friedel's whole body was in shock. Her very bones ached at the mere idea of being separated from her twin.

She was so upset, she didn't notice when the Z names came to an end and the officer started on another list of names, not in any order. Suddenly the loudspeaker blasted out, '*Friedel Rosenthal.*'

Friedel gave a little shriek. Gina's hand squeezed hers. Both sisters almost wept with relief. They would remain together, they would survive together. They would continue to keep one another's hearts strong.

CHAPTER SIXTEEN

The Pits of Turkheim

Yet another journey. Yet another train. Yet another dark, closed wagon filled with cold, hungry, exhausted people. The cold was the worst. Then the hunger. The women in the wagons got a ladle of soup each per day, and that was all.

Sitting close together to fend off the cold, Friedel and Gina tried to cheer each other up. In their imaginations they drew pictures of what things would be like once all this was over. What would their lives become, when they were free? What would they do? Their thoughts swirled, but always came back to one thing – food. Between them the sisters conjured up the feasts they would gather, the long-lost brothers and sisters who would sit down to enjoy it with them. And of course the warm, bright homes in which it would all happen.

The shared dreams helped to keep them going.

Day after day the train rolled slowly on or sat still. Repeatedly it was held up by bombs wrecking the railway line somewhere up ahead. At one city in the middle of Germany, the train stopped for nine whole days. American planes had bombed the rail junctions there, and no trains could go through until it was all repaired.

Friedel and Gina's wagon was guarded the whole time by a single German soldier armed with a rifle. He sat near the door, and looked so utterly miserable that Friedel *almost* felt sorry for him. Especially as the corner right beside him was where the women went to the toilet.

The journey from Bergen-Belsen had gone on for two entire weeks when the train stopped once more. This time they had reached their destination, a small town called Burgau, deep in the south of Germany, in the region called Bavaria.

Bavaria is one of the loveliest places in Europe. A land of forests, hills and mountain valleys, dotted with farms, fairy-tale castles and pretty villages. It was also a land of Nazism. Hitler loved Bavaria. Its main city, Munich, was where he had first started his rise to power.

Back in 1933, when the Nazi government began, the SS had chosen this region for the first big concentration camp. They created it just outside a small town near Munich called Dachau.

Friedel and Gina had been little children at the time, but they remembered hearing people talk about Dachau as a place of terror. Not only Jews, but everyone who had reason to fear the Nazis, or who dared to oppose them, shuddered when they heard that name. Over the years since, the Dachau camp had grown vast, and sprouted dozens of smaller camps scattered throughout the region. And each of those smaller camps had grown its own crop of even smaller camps. There were now over a hundred and eighty of them, all under the control of Dachau. The camp at Burgau was one of them.

The town of Burgau was a beautiful little place. A huddle of brightly painted houses and churches, nestled among wooded hills. Right beside it, the SS had built their thoroughly hideous little concentration camp. It housed the prisoners who worked in the aeroplane factory, which was nearby.

Once more Friedel and Gina and their friends had to get used to new surroundings. Their names and details were taken down again, and they were each given prisoner numbers, which had to be displayed on their uniforms.

The camp only had a few barracks, all newly built. They had the usual bunks inside, so at least the women wouldn't have to sleep in a heap on the floor. After the wagon, it was a relief to be in a room that didn't stink like a sewer.

With aching limbs, the women and girls climbed into their bunks, packed in like sardines, and slept.

* * *

The morning routine was a familiar one. Up before dawn to assemble for roll call. Hot acorn coffee was doled out into their tin cups. And then something new. Instead of a long march to work, the prisoners were led to a little fleet of buses.

As they drove out through the gate, Friedel and Gina sat in a trance-like state. It was so weird to be

sitting in comfort, watching the outside world go by, lit by the glimmers of dawn. They gazed in wonder at the pretty houses. Inside each one a family lived, probably still sleeping. Happy people – mums and dads, kids and grandparents. Folk who went out to work or to school and came home to a fire in the hearth and food on the table. To most people this was all normal, ordinary. But to Friedel and Gina it seemed like fantasy from a realm of fairy tales and dreams.

After a couple of kilometres the convoy of buses left the highway and drove into a pine forest. The factory was buried deep among the trees and well camouflaged to conceal it from Allied bombers. Inside, Nazi engineers and their workers built high-tech jet fighters.

At last they reached the factory. The buses emptied out, and the prisoners found themselves looking at a sweep of wide concrete steps, leading up to a kind of fortified entrance. Across it, huge camouflage nets were draped.

Inside was a factory where sleek aeroplanes were being assembled. They were incredible things, with a shark-like shape and no propellers. At that time, there was nothing like them in any air force in the world. Hitler believed that these and other advanced weapons could still win the war for the Nazis.

The workers were a mixture of civilians and prisoners. All the prisoners were starved and skinny, their striped uniforms hanging loosely. The new arrivals were given unskilled work to do around the factory. It was every bit as tedious and unpleasant as the Hasag factory.

After twelve hours of toil, it was back to the buses for the drive to the camp.

That evening, they received their only meal of the day. A great steel cauldron of miserable stew was brought out. As it sloshed into their bowls, Friedel and Gina looked at it – a few bits of scraggy meat and chunks of potato floating in warm water.

The next day was a repeat of the one before, including the bus ride through dreamland and the watery stew. The day after that was the same again. And then it stopped. On the fourth day, the prisoners were left to their own devices. There was no journey, and no work. They had no idea why.

A rumour went around that the Germans couldn't get the parts for their jet aeroplanes any more, because of the war. The British and American bombers had devastated Germany's industry and railways, and all kinds of supplies were just about impossible to get. Day after day there was nothing for the prisoners to do.

Less than three weeks after they arrived in Burgau, they were told they were being moved yet again. Another train. Another freight wagon. Another journey in darkness and misery. And yet another godforsaken camp. At least this time the journey was a short one.

* * *

The new camp was at a place called Turkheim, only about fifty kilometres from Burgau. Like Burgau, it was part of the Dachau system.

Turkheim concentration camp was far more basic than any other Friedel and Gina had seen. The SS had created thousands of camps, large and small, across Germany and Poland and every other country they had occupied. The one at Turkheim was very small indeed. Although it certainly wasn't the worst concentration camp, it was probably the most primitive. It didn't even have barrack blocks.

When the women from Czestochowa entered the camp, they were puzzled by what they saw. There was a simple dirt road through the middle. On either side, where you'd normally have barrack blocks, there were things that were the shape of low, ridged tents, but made of wood. They were very low – only a metre or so from ground level to the top of the roof. Each one was covered over with earth and had a door at one end.

The SS guards and kapos herded the prisoners towards them. Friedel and Gina had to bend almost double to get through the door.

Inside they saw that it was a deep pit dug in the ground. The roof was made from flimsy-looking beams and plywood. These pit-barracks had been built in a great hurry. Although they were less than a year old, the roofs leaked, the wood was rotting, and they were infested with rats.

The pits were dark even in the daytime. There were no electric lights, and not even an oil lamp or candle. The only light came from a little square window in the door. In this deep gloom the prisoners lived night and day. There was no work routine at Turkheim, and instead they were roused as usual in the dawn light for roll call, then sent back into their pits. The SS didn't seem to know what to do with them.

Weeks passed by in this way. April came, so at least the weather was getting warmer. Living in these pits in the depths of winter must have been unimaginably awful.

Out in the world, Nazi Germany was in its dying days. It clung on only because of Hitler's fanatical determination. Even now he believed he could win the war, and the SS shared his wild delusions. They went on fighting, and went on tormenting and killing the inmates of the camps.

At this point, most other Germans were either surrendering or simply fighting for their lives and homes. Many of them no longer even cared about Hitler or Nazism; they cared only about defending Germany itself. The delightful villages of Bavaria would soon be overrun by American tanks and soldiers. Many would become battlegrounds. All across Germany, American, British, Canadian, Polish, French, Russian, Ukrainian and a dozen other countries' soldiers were whittling the German armies down.

The end was only a handful of weeks away. But for those in the concentration camps, freedom in a week might be too late. Most of them had only a few days' worth of strength left in them. For some, it was a matter of hours.

One of those was Gina Rosenthal.

* * *

Gina had never felt so ill. It was a bit like flu – she was weak, aching, sweating and shivering. But she knew from seeing other prisoners with the same symptoms that it wasn't flu. It was the beginning of typhus.

To add to Gina's misery, she had a painful lump on her gum. Touching it with her fingertip sent bolts of agony through her skull. She needed to go to the camp doctor but was too frightened. Just as it had been in the ghetto, if you admitted you were sick, the SS were likely to hurry along your death.

Gina put up with the pain as best she could throughout the night, but by morning it was unbearable. She talked it over with Friedel.

'I can't stand it,' she said. 'I'm going to the doctor.'

Friedel was horrified, but she could see how much pain Gina was in. It tore at her heart. 'Are you sure?'

Gina nodded. After roll call, she walked unsteadily to the shabby hut that passed for a medical station and lined up with the other people who'd become desperate enough to seek help here. The doctor looked them over one by one. SS doctors were notorious. Many of them weren't even qualified, and most regarded sick prisoners as problems to get rid of rather than as patients to treat. Some even used the prisoners for medical experiments.

Peering into Gina's mouth, the doctor grunted. 'Just an abscess,' he muttered. 'Why are you wasting my time with this? Here, open up.' Gripping Gina's jaw, he pulled her mouth wide and reached inside with a scalpel blade.

Gina felt a quick stab as he sliced the lump open. The pain in her gum flared up, but then started to fade away. A sour, metallic taste filled her mouth.

'There,' said the doctor. 'That's drained out the muck. But it's still infected. Don't go asking for any medications because I haven't got any. It might get better on its own. Now, get out of my sight.' As Gina was turning to leave, the doctor said, 'Wait!' He peered at her. 'You don't look well. What symptoms do you have?'

Gina's heart thumped. Her skin, sweaty with fever, turned icy. 'Nothing, sir. I'm fine.'

The doctor's eyes narrowed, but then he lost interest and turned to his next patient. Gina walked away, sighing with relief.

* * *

THE PITS OF TURKHEIM

Friedel sat alone in the darkness of the pit. Gina had gone to see the doctor without eating her ration of bread. Friedel was keeping it for her. Minutes went by, and Friedel's hunger kept telling her to eat Gina's bread. It was as if the hunger had become a monster that lived inside her. *Go on*, it whispered. *You need that bread. It's right there, waiting to be eaten.*

The hunger surged through every part of her, pushing her, tempting her to pop the stale bread in her mouth. It took hold of her hand and tried to force the bread towards her lips. She pushed it back down, making herself put the bread in her pocket, out of sight.

Her willpower had conquered the hunger – but for how long? If Gina didn't return soon, Friedel feared that it wouldn't win eventually. She was ashamed that such thoughts could even enter her head. To eat her twin sister's only food? How could she even think it?

Hunger is natural. It keeps us alive. But if it isn't satisfied, and if it turns into starvation, it becomes an evil thing. If it grows strong enough, it can make a person do things they would never do in their right mind. Sometimes terrible things, sometimes just foolish and dangerous.

When Gina returned, Friedel gave her the bread. It dismayed Friedel every time she looked at her twin how painfully skinny she'd become. Of course, Friedel was starved too, but she couldn't see herself as Gina must see her.

That evening, when they trooped out to roll call, Friedel had to help Gina stay on her feet. The typhus was getting worse. Gina was so weak and dizzy she could hardly stand upright. The kapos watched the prisoners but didn't pay very close attention to them. Hopefully they wouldn't notice.

There were two kapos in their pit barrack – Rebeka and Hilde. Their personalities were as different as could be. Hilde was unusually nice for a kapo, a bit like a mother to the prisoners. But Rebeka was horrible.

After roll call that evening, cauldrons of watery stew were carried into the barrack for the prisoners' evening meal. Kapo Rebeka stood watching it being doled out. As always, a prisoner had been given the job of ladling the slop into everyone's bowls. Gina and Friedel had got separated in the mass filing down through the doorway, and Gina got to the front of the queue first. The prisoner serving her turned away for a moment and left the ladle hanging on the edge of the cauldron. Gina wasn't thinking straight: hunger and the fever had scrambled her brain. She reached for the ladle and helped herself to the stew.

That was something you just didn't do. Rebeka's anger boiled up. 'What d'you think you're doing, you pig? You think this is a buffet?' She lashed out with her fist, hitting Gina in the chest. Gina staggered and almost fell down.

Friedel came down the steps just in time to see Rebeka thump Gina again and again, shouting furiously at her.

'Leave her alone!' Friedel yelled. Shoving her way through the crowd, she threw herself at the kapo. She pummelled her with her fists and clawed at her. Rebeka was so shocked she cowered away and didn't try to fight back.

For a moment, Friedel and Rebeka stood glaring at one another. Everyone waited to see what would happen next.

In the old days of the camps, Friedel's reward for such an outrageous act would have been a severe beating from the kapos. But things weren't quite the same any more. Every kapo had always known that the prisoners hated them, and there was always the risk of the people they abused taking revenge. Now that the end of the Nazis' power was in sight, perhaps Rebeka felt that she was less safe than she used to be. As she stared at Friedel, she was surrounded by prisoners who all had reasons to pay back the hurts she'd inflicted on them.

Pulling herself together, Rebeka turned back to the cauldron and continued with the serving. She had chosen to pretend that Friedel's outburst hadn't happened.

At least, that was how it seemed. But Rebeka was determined to get her own back. The next morning, Rebeka was in a foul mood. As she and Hilde roused the prisoners out for roll call, she shoved them hard – towards the door, up the steps, and out into the little square. Friedel was one of the ones she shoved hardest. Buoyed up by the previous night's incident, Friedel shoved Rebeka back.

Again Rebeka did nothing, just glared at her.

At the end of roll call, as the prisoners were about to be sent back to the barrack, the SS sergeant in charge suddenly called out, 'Would the prisoner who hit a kapo last night step forward?'

Friedel froze. She glanced left and right, hoping that perhaps some other prisoner had hit some other kapo and was about to come forward. Or maybe a part of her hoped that someone else would confess to her own crime. There was silence. Nobody moved. They all knew who the sergeant meant. Friedel felt as if a hundred pairs of eyes were boring into her.

With an effort, she raised her hand.

'Come forward,' the sergeant ordered.

Friedel left the lines and stood out in front of the assembly. She saw Rebeka staring at her with malice in her eyes.

The sergeant said to Rebeka. 'Okay, now hit her as hard as she hit you.'

Rebeka gave a smile as she came towards Friedel. With a grunt, she flung out her fist, hitting Friedel in the face as hard as she could. Stars flicked in front of Friedel's eyes and bolts of blinding pain rattled around in her skull.

The sergeant looked on. 'Hmph,' he said with a raised eyebrow. 'I wouldn't have hit her quite *that* hard.'

After this, the prisoners were sent back into the barrack for their breakfast. All Friedel's attention was on nursing her pounding head. She hadn't hit Rebeka anywhere near as hard as that, even after what she'd done to Gina. The worst thing was that Rebeka was Jewish, like the rest of them. Friedel couldn't understand how people could behave like this to their own kind.

Her friend Franka saw that Friedel's rage was still burning. 'Be careful,' she said. 'Rebeka can do worse than that to you. Don't push her.'

Franka was right. As difficult as it was, Friedel let her anger simmer down. Strength and patience would get them through this – anger and violence would not.

* * *

With each day that passed, Gina's typhus got worse, and soon she couldn't even stand up any more. It became impossible to hide how sick she was. Rebeka noticed, and that meant that the SS doctor found out too.

Typhus had always been a problem in every concentration camp. Lack of medical care and sanitation caused it. Now, extreme overcrowding increased the infections. Turkheim was no exception, and the awful, filthy conditions in the pit barracks made the epidemic worse.

There were so many prisoners sick with it that the camp doctor had them all moved into a single pit barrack together. He called it 'quarantine' – a way to keep the disease away from other prisoners. But it felt as if it had a much more sinister purpose.

When they came to take Gina away to the typhus barrack, there was nothing Friedel could do. Her heart filled with despair as her sister was carried away, so delirious that she hardly knew what was happening.

For the first time in her life, Friedel was alone.

* * *

Friedel sat with her tin cup, staring into the syrupy acorn coffee. She felt wretched, filthy, desperate.

She recalled the old life, all the way back to her earliest memories. The shop in Marken Street, the lovely apartment above, the happy family. The fresh coffee, the aroma of sweets and cakes and tobacco, the friendly chatter of the customers. It had all been so *clean*, so *comfortable*. Friedel longed to be clean again. Her body was grimy and sore, her hair tangled and matted with greasy, gritty dirt.

Was it possible to wash your hair with acorn coffee? She'd heard that you could use proper coffee in that way. Maybe this kind would work too. She was desperate enough to try it. She poured the stuff on to her hair, and began to scrub. Once it was all rubbed in, she went to the washroom at the end of the camp and ran her head under cold water.

It seemed to work. A little, at least.

Feeling slightly better, she went back to the pit. While her hair dried in the cool air, her thoughts returned again to the old days. She remembered setting out for their first day at school, a whole lifetime ago. How innocent she and Gina had been then. Friedel remembered laughing at the mix-up with the coats, Mum smiling delightedly and getting Hans to fetch the camera. Friedel could see that photo in her mind. She'd looked at it so many times, it was as clear to her now as if she held it in her hand. Friedel saw her own face, with that grin. And Gina's softer smile, her eyes thoughtful. It burned Friedel's heart that there was no way back to that day, to that moment, to that happy life.

Suddenly, she got up and felt her way through the darkness to the barrack door. Up the steps and out into the daylight she went. Quickly she made her way between the barracks to the one where the typhus patients were.

There were no kapos about, so Friedel peered in through the little window in the door. She could just make out Gina lying near the foot of the steps. Her face was a pale blur in the gloom.

'Gina?' she said. There was no response. 'Gina, it's me!' she called, louder this time. Still no sign that Gina could hear her. No sign of life. Was she already dead?

Carefully Friedel edged the door open and called out again. To her relief, this time Gina stirred.

'Gina, it's me! It's Friedel. I've come to see you.'

Her sister's eyes half-opened blearily and blinked. 'Hmm?'

'How are you feeling? Any better?'

Gina mumbled something that Friedel couldn't make out, then turned her head away. Her face was drenched in sweat. 'Mum?' she muttered. 'Mum, I don't feel well.' She was delirious, her mind wandering in half-dreams. Friedel's heart twisted in pain.

A woman's voice barked, 'Hey, what are you doing there?'

Friedel nearly jumped out of her skin. She turned to find a kapo glaring at her.

'This is a typhus barrack. You shouldn't be here. Get back to your own barrack, now!'

'But my sister –'

'*Now!*' The kapo moved towards her.

Friedel jumped up and ran back to her barrack. In the reeking gloom, she sat down by the wall, crying.

Feeling a hand on her arm, she looked up to find Franka watching her with worry in her eyes. Franka smiled.

'You know, I heard the Americans are very close now.'

Friedel sniffed and wiped her eyes. 'How close? They've been saying that for weeks.'

'Well, now they're saying you can hear the guns if you listen carefully.' Franka's voice lowered. 'I also heard we're going to be evacuated.'

'Again,' said Friedel.

'Yes, again.'

Another prisoner overheard their conversation and chimed in. 'I hear they're going to finish off the sick before we leave.'

Friedel stared at her. '*What?*'

Franka tried to shush the woman with a frantic gesture, but she continued regardless. 'The SS are going to take all the typhus lot out in the woods and shoot them.' Like an unstoppable juggernaut, the woman ploughed on: 'Or set fire to the sick barracks. One or the other. Poor souls.'

Friedel stared sightlessly into the darkness, numbed and paralysed by dread. Of all the ways she had foreseen their ordeal ending, it had never been like this. To be separated from her twin right at the end. To die separately. Friedel couldn't stand it. She *wouldn't* stand it. It couldn't be allowed to happen.

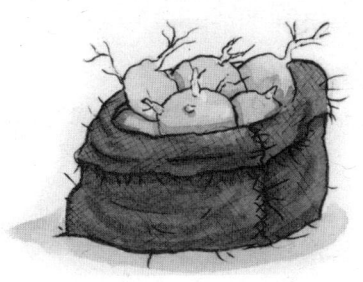

CHAPTER SEVENTEEN

Evacuation

Overnight, the rumours turned into realities. Every soul in Turkheim now knew that the Americans were only days away. The SS were going to evacuate the camp at any moment, and it became ever more certain that they were planning to kill off anyone who was too sick to be moved.

Friedel sat with her piece of bread and bowl of stew. She toyed with the bread. Her hunger, which had been a constant part of her for years, was just about all gone. Everyone was saying that the sick were going to be disposed of tomorrow.

How could this happen? How could it happen *now*? After all she and Gina had been through together! From the bewilderment of their first day at school to the hateful Brownshirts in the streets

of Dusseldorf. From the city prison to the stables in Zbaszyn. From the orphanage in Lodz to the ghetto of Czestochowa. From the selections to the Hasag camp. And all the way from there to here, to the pits of Turkheim. And the train journeys – good grief, the train journeys! Days upon suffocating days in those foul, dark wagons.

Piece by piece the twins' family had been taken from them. Layer by layer, the love that cushioned them against the world had been peeled away. Hans, Max, Martha, Bernard, Father, Mum. And now Gina.

Enough! Friedel wouldn't let it end this way. Even with all the power of the Nazis against her, she simply wouldn't allow this world to swallow up Gina – her twin, her other half.

That evening, after dark, Friedel went up the steps and peered cautiously out. There was nobody nearby. She crept outside, quietly pulling the door shut behind her. Flitting across the camp road, she felt her way to the typhus barrack and, crouching down near the corner of the low roof, she looked around. A couple of guards were patrolling along the fence, just a few yards away. All Friedel could make out was their starlit outlines against the black background and their heavy tread on the bare earth.

Waiting until they'd gone by, Friedel inched her way to the barrack door. She prayed with all her heart that Gina was still in the same place, just inside. In the pitch black, it would be impossible to find her without waking everyone, including the kapos.

The door made a gut-churning creak as Friedel pulled it open. Prickles of fear ran all over her skin, and she stopped, holding her breath. All she could hear was the heavy, troubled breathing of the sick prisoners in the barrack. The creak had probably sounded much louder in her head than it really was.

Inside, it felt as if the air was humming with deadly typhus germs. Trying not to breathe, Friedel went down the last few steps to the first straw bed on the right.

'Gina?' she whispered.

No response. Friedel didn't dare speak any louder, so she reached out and felt for the person on the bed. Her hand found a shoulder, and she shook it gently.

'Hngh?' the person grunted.

Friedel's body tingled with relief. It was Gina's voice. 'Gina, listen, I'm getting you out of here.'

'Hmm?' Gina's voice was weak and slurred.

Friedel didn't have time to explain. She raised Gina to a sitting position. Wrapping her arms round her, Friedel wrestled her to her feet. With Gina's arm hooked round her neck and gripped firmly, Friedel began helping her up the steps. Her sister didn't have the strength to walk. It was like hauling a sack of soil – if sacks of soil could groan alarmingly. Every sound threatened to alert the kapos.

With extreme difficulty, Friedel got Gina to the door. Checking that nobody was around, she helped her up the last step. Once they were on level ground, the going was a bit easier. Looking and listening all the way, Friedel got her sister to their own barrack. Another exhausting struggle through the door and down the steps, and they were safely inside, sealed within the darkness of their own pit.

Friedel sat back and considered the seriousness of what she had done. She was risking her own life, and Gina's, and those of all their friends. If she was caught, there would be punishment, perhaps for all of them. But she didn't care. She had Gina, and there was no way the Nazis or the typhus germs were going to take her away.

* * *

When morning came, a strange mood had settled over the SS guards. They were nervous, excitable. Many were drunk. They had put their hearts and souls – and even their very lives – into Hitler's great project. And now it was all falling into ruin. Some despaired, some were furious, a few still believed that Hitler would win.

They were in just the mood to turn the prisoners' worst fears into reality. Hearing a loud disturbance going on outside, Friedel and a couple of her friends went to the window in their barrack door. The SS and kapos had surrounded the typhus barrack. They flung open the door and started forcing the sick people outside. Some were still able to walk by themselves, but many staggered and had to be helped along by the stronger ones. All of them were far too weak to resist.

Friedel watched the people being herded along the dirt road towards the gate. Eventually they were out of sight, and silence fell over the camp. It went on for a very long time. Friedel began to wonder if she'd been wrong to worry. Perhaps the sick people were being evacuated first? Perhaps they would be taken on ahead to some other camp? But she had lived under the Nazis long enough to know that it was a vain hope.

As if to underline her thoughts, the silence was suddenly shattered by a loud crash of gunfire. It came from the direction of the woods. Hush fell again ... and then another crackle of gunshots, like the sound of a firework display in the distance.

Friedel sat hunched, hugging her knees, trying not to hear. Each bang was the brutal full stop at the end of a person's life. That could have been Gina out there.

As soon as the dreadful noises came to an end, the SS returned. They were in a frantic mood, as if the shooting had woken something in them. Suddenly there was chaos. They hurried through the camp, shouting, 'Out, out, all of you out!' Barrack doors were flung open. Kapos and guards yelled into the darkness inside, 'Everyone out now! Form up into groups of five and come outside.'

Kapo Rebeka came in and announced, 'We're all being evacuated to the east. Come on, outside now in fives! Assemble at the cookhouse. You'll get a sausage and loaf of bread for each group for the journey.'

Friedel's suspicions rose immediately. She had vivid memories of selections, and of the empty promises the Nazis made. While the other women got together in groups of five, Friedel explained to Gina what was going on.

'I don't trust this,' she said. 'We mustn't be tempted by the food, no matter how hungry we are, you understand?' Gina was delirious still, but she seemed to get what Friedel was saying. 'We've been hungry before, Gina, you and I. *So* hungry. We can starve some more. Let's not be tempted by their loaf and sausage. We'll wait and hang back. Maybe the Americans will get here soon, before the Nazis do whatever they're planning to do to us.'

A long queue formed at the place where the food was being doled out. Friedel and Gina went slowly, so that they'd be at the very end of the line. Gina seemed to be recovering a little. With help from Friedel, she could just about stay on her feet. She was so thin, so hollowed out, it broke Friedel's heart to look at her.

The queue moved forward, and as it did so, Friedel and Gina hung further and further back, until they weren't even part of it. At last, when the main gate opened and the prisoners began to march out on to the road, the twins were among the people left behind. Only about half the camp was leaving, and most of the SS went to guard them on the march. There were no trains to take them wherever they were going. They'd be walking all the way. To Friedel's relief, there were no sounds of gunfire, so maybe the sausages and bread hadn't been a trap after all.

That evening, the camp felt like a different place. The kapos and the remaining SS guards no longer bothered to do their jobs. The only thing keeping the prisoners in was the barbed wire.

Friedel, Franka and a couple of other friends decided to mount a raid on the camp stores. They'd starved all day. Like Friedel, they'd distrusted the food being handed out, and now was their chance to do something about their hunger.

The storeroom wasn't exactly well-stocked. There were some sacks of potatoes, and that was about all.

'Let's make latkes,' said Friedel.

'With what?' said one of her friends. 'Just raw potatoes?'

Latkes are a traditional Jewish food. They're a type of fritter, made from fried grated potato. Sometimes cheese is added. Friedel and her friends didn't have any cheese, or a frying pan, or even a grater.

'Well, we can try.' Friedel picked up an empty tin and a nail. She punched holes in the tin from the inside. There – now she had something to grate the potato with.

The other girls copied her, and soon they had a good heap of grated potato, which they moulded into patties. With nothing to hold them together, the latkes were rather loose and fragile, but not bad considering. They got a fire going in the storeroom stove and balanced the latkes on the hot chimney pipe at the back.

Even though they were nothing like real latkes, the

crumbly lumps of singed potato were a feast for the starving girls. Even Gina managed to enjoy them.

'They'll probably take us out tomorrow,' said Franka. 'We won't get away with this again.'

'What if there's a selection?' said Judyta.

They glanced at one another. None of them looked healthy enough to pass a selection any more, and they needed to do something to change that. Franka had managed to scrounge a used-up end of lipstick. It was a treasured possession. Carefully they rubbed it into each other's cheeks to try and make them look more healthy.

Friedel remembered trying the same trick with Mum. It was a desperate, hopeless thing to do, and it hadn't saved Mum. But it was impossible not to at least try.

* * *

There wasn't a selection. At least, not yet. When the prisoners were called out to assemble, it was the same as the day before. They were given a loaf and sausage for each group of five. This time the twins and their friends joined the queue and accepted their ration of food. Then the remaining SS guards surrounded them and began to march them out through the gate.

It opened on to a narrow country lane, with woods on both sides. Friedel looked at the trees and felt a strong temptation to just make a run for it. But the guards were watchful, their rifles ready in their hands.

She said quietly to Franka, 'If we get a chance, we have to try to escape.'

Franka glanced at the guards. 'That's a big *if*,' she said doubtfully. Apart from anything else, Franka was Polish, so this was a foreign country to her. The same was true of most of their old friends from Czestochowa. Of those who weren't Polish, some were Romanian. Only a handful were German.

Friedel guessed her friend's fears. 'It's OK. Gina and I speak German. Maybe we can pass for locals, or just hide. We can live off the land.'

'It's April,' said Franka. 'There won't be any crops or anything.'

'We'll find something. It's got to be better than the food in the camp.'

The long, straggling column of prisoners passed by the village of Turkheim and continued on. The SS were driving them northeast. None of the prisoners knew where they were going. Some other camp, they assumed – if they were lucky. Or a grave somewhere in the woods if their worst fears came true.

All the small camps near to Turkheim were also emptying out on to the roads. Altogether, 15,000 prisoners were on the march. Only a few months ago, those camps had contained twice that number. The ones on the march were those who had survived the typhus and the shootings.

From time to time, the distant drone of aeroplanes could be heard. American fighter planes were patrolling all over the area, looking for German targets to attack. If they saw a train, a convoy of trucks or a column of German soldiers, the gleaming silver planes would swoop, shrieking, from the skies. Their machine-gun bullets raked the ground, destroying anything in their path. Some of the pilots were so eager to kill Nazis that they didn't always look carefully before they attacked.

Friedel and Franka trudged along, tired, wondering how long they could keep going. Gina was between them. She could just about stay upright and put one foot in front of the other, but she was weak and dizzy. They helped her as best they could.

The buzz of planes caught Friedel's ears, suddenly growing louder. The narrow road was lined on both sides by forest, which deadened the sound a bit, but the change in volume was clear. She glanced at Franka.

'I hear it,' Franka said nervously. 'They're heading this way.'

The buzz turned rapidly into the tearing roar of engines. The American fighters came diving down, skimming above the treetops, turning to line up with the road. Their wings sparkled with flame, and a spattering curtain of dust and grit flew up along the road.

EVACUATION

The column of prisoners erupted with screams of terror. Some were hit by the hail of bullets. Most flung themselves towards the roadside ditches. The SS guards were too busy saving themselves to pay any attention to the prisoners. Pulling Gina with them, Friedel and Franka leapt into the ditch and squashed themselves down, trying to melt into the earth. Several of their friends jumped in beside them. Luckily, none of them had been hit.

It only lasted a few seconds. There was a faint patter as the grit settled back down. In the distance, the fighters' engines shrank to a faint hum.

'This is it!' said Friedel. 'Come on!'

Snatching Gina by the wrist, Friedel scrambled out of the ditch and plunged headlong into the forest. She could hear her friends running behind her. Branches whipped at their faces, roots tripped them up, but they kept on running.

After a while they stopped, gasping for breath, their lungs aching. They couldn't be sure how far they'd gone. Then they heard the SS guards getting people marching again, yelling '*Schnell! Schnell!*' – 'Quickly! Quickly!' It was much too close for comfort.

Moving more carefully, Friedel, Gina, Franka and the others ventured deeper into the wood. It was late afternoon, the sun was sinking and a gloom was growing among the trees. When they stopped to rest again, the girls could hear voices all around. Most were speaking in Polish. It seemed that other prisoners had taken advantage of the chaos to make their own bids for freedom.

Too exhausted to try to get any further, the girls lay down and slept under the rustling roof of the trees. For almost all of them it was their first night's sleep in freedom for four years.

CHAPTER EIGHTEEN

The Second House

The forest was dripping and cold when they woke. It had drizzled all night, and their clothes were damp.

To Friedel's delight, Gina was starting to feel a little stronger now – just enough to walk without help. That was lucky, because Friedel herself was starting to feel weaker. Not typhus, she was sure. Her stomach hurt. 'Those latkes,' she said. 'I'm sure it was those.'

'What do we do now?' said Franka.

Gina shrugged. 'Head into Turkheim village, I guess? It's the nearest place.'

Friedel agreed. 'The other direction is just Nazis everywhere. The Americans might be in Turkheim by now.'

They gathered their spirits, shook the rainwater out of their hair, and began picking their way through the woods. They had little sense of direction among the trees, but they figured they were heading more or less southwest. It shouldn't be far to the village. The march from the camp had been so slow that they hadn't gone more than a dozen or so kilometres before the planes attacked.

Once they were out of the trees they found a lane heading in the right direction. As they were approaching the village, they came to a farmhouse. Set back a little way from the road, it was a typical small Bavarian farmhouse. A low, neat dwelling, painted white, with a little wooden barn built on at one end.

'Maybe we could get help here?' Franka suggested.

The other girls agreed. The people in the house would be Germans, of course, but if they didn't suspect that the girls were Jewish, they might be willing to help. Did local people know about the nearby camp? Would they guess that the girls were prisoners there? Everyone looked to Friedel and Gina, the only ones who could speak German.

'All right,' said Friedel.

As she put her hand on the gate to open it, something made her stop. She looked again at the house. There was something about it she didn't like. She couldn't tell why – it was a harmless, pleasant-looking place, but it gave Friedel a nasty, creepy chill down her spine. She studied the blank, dark windows. It was as if unseen eyes were watching her, hostile and malevolent. Was she imagining it? Of course she must be . . . but . . .

'No,' she said. 'Not here.'

'Why not? What's wrong with it?'

'Nothing,' said Friedel. 'I mean ... never mind. We'll try the next one.'

As they walked on, Friedel glanced back uneasily at the little white house. It looked so innocent, yet she felt sure it was watching her with bad intent.

A little way further along the road, they came to another farmhouse. Larger than the first, it was also white and had a barn built on to it. Friedel thought it looked quite beautiful, nestled among the trees and fields.

'Can we try here?' said Gina.

Friedel nodded. 'Come on.'

Leaving their friends at the gate, the twins ventured in. As they did, the farmhouse door opened, and a middle-aged woman came out carrying a basket of laundry. She paused, startled by the sight of two skinny, scruffy girls on her garden path. Looking at their striped coats, she clearly guessed that they'd come from the concentration camp. She probably also guessed that they were Jews.

'Please,' said Friedel. 'We're sorry to bother you. Do you have any food you could spare?'

As the woman opened her mouth to reply, a young man came round from the back of the house. A German soldier. A Nazi. His arm was in a bloodstained sling. He stopped and stared at the two girls, and they stared at him. *This is it*, Friedel thought. *We're done for.*

Quickly, the woman put down her laundry basket and gestured to Friedel and Gina. 'Come quickly. In the house. Come on, hurry now!'

The twins followed her, eyeing the soldier warily. He made no move towards them, and in a moment they were inside the house.

They found themselves in a pleasant, warm farmhouse kitchen. Sitting at the table was a teenage boy, who they guessed was the woman's son. He looked at them in surprise, but didn't seem hostile.

The woman encouraged the girls to sit at the table too and have a little food. 'Don't be frightened,' she said. 'We won't harm you.'

Her son said, 'The Americans will be here by tonight, I bet you.' To their surprise he smiled, as if he was looking forward to it. 'Look,' he said, and took out a well-worn map stuck to a board. It had little coloured pins all over it. He pointed to them enthusiastically. 'Here are the front lines, you see? Our army is retreating here and here. They can't hang on. The Americans will push right through. They're bound to enter the village by tonight.'

Friedel and Gina didn't know what to make of all this. Not just the boy's map, but the boy himself, his mother, this place. There was a crucifix on the wall, and pictures of Jesus and the Virgin Mary. This was obviously a very strongly Catholic home. Friedel and Gina had learned the hard way to be wary of any Germans who weren't fellow

Jews, and it was hard to figure out what the woman and her son were thinking. Why were they being so kind? It made no sense to the twins. Friedel glanced nervously towards the door, wondering about the German soldier they'd seen.

The woman seemed to guess her thoughts. 'Don't worry about him. Poor lad's wounded and had enough of fighting for the Nazis. He's laying low here ready to surrender when the Americans come.'

'My father's gone into the village,' said the boy, and added, 'Our name is Mayer. I'm Carl.'

'I'm Friedel.'

'I'm Regina. We're sisters. Twins. We're from Dusseldorf.' She glanced at Friedel. 'A long time ago.'

Mrs Mayer smiled and said, 'It's pleasant to meet you, Friedel and Regina. When my husband comes back we'll try to work it out so that you can stay.'

Gina said, 'We have friends that came with us. Six of us in all. We escaped. Can they . . .?' She hesitated.

Mrs Mayer was frowning. 'We might be able to fit you two in, if my husband says it's all right, but no more than that. I'm sorry. You'll have to tell them to look elsewhere. They'll find somewhere in the village, I'm sure. We have a spare room. It used to be the maid's room, but she's gone now. You can have that.'

There was nothing to do but take this family on trust and choose to believe that their kindness was genuine.

It was only fair, since Mrs Mayer and her son seemed to be taking the twins on trust.

'I should explain how we came to be here,' Friedel said. She described the concentration camp, the pit barracks, the evacuation and the Death March, and finally their escape.

Mrs Mayer listened intently. She was upset but didn't seem surprised. She clearly knew about the camp and the conditions inside it. Turkheim was a small village, the kind of place where talk gets around and nothing stays hidden for long, if at all. The local people had seen prisoners arriving, heard the gunfire a few days ago, and had seen, through the barbed wire, the pit barracks and the wretched souls who lived in them.

'We'll feed you,' said Mrs Mayer. 'But you've been starved, I can see, so if you eat too much it'll make you ill.' She thought for a moment. 'Baked potatoes,' she said. 'Yes, I'll put some potatoes in to bake. And some nice warm milk.'

Friedel and Gina's eyes prickled with tears. It had been so long since they'd received kindness. Sitting there at the scrubbed table in that nice, clean kitchen they were painfully aware of the filthy state they were in. Out of the corner of her eye Friedel noticed that Gina was trying to brush away the lice that were crawling out of her coat sleeve. Friedel kicked her under the table. *Stop making it so obvious*, she thought.

Once they'd drunk a little warm milk, Mrs Mayer took the girls upstairs and showed them the maid's bedroom. It was a simple enough room, furnished in Bavarian style, with a hefty, carved wooden bedstead. Like the rest of the house it was spotlessly clean and tidy. The twins' eyes were so used to miserable conditions that it seemed like a princess's chamber in a palace.

Looking at the bed, with its beautiful eiderdown and white pillows, they were even more aware of how filthy they both were.

'Thank you,' said Friedel. 'But we can't sleep in your nice bed. We're just . . .' She trailed off. 'Is it possible for us to have a wash?'

'Of course,' said Mrs Mayer. 'I'll see to it.'

As nice as the house was, it was very old-fashioned, even for those days. There was no bathroom, and no hot running water. The family washed at the sink and bathed in a metal tub that hung from a hook in a cupboard. Mrs Mayer fetched it and placed it in front of the bedroom fireplace. Then she made several trips up and down the stairs with copper kettles of water she'd boiled on the stove. There was no proper soap, because of the war. Like with the fake coffee in the camps, German people had fake soap, made with clay and cheap chemicals. But it got them clean.

The feeling was incredible. They hadn't had hot water on their skin for years. The warmth of it felt alive and friendly, like a hug.

Once they'd washed, Mrs Mayer fetched them some clean clothes. She took their camp uniforms, holding them at arms' length, her nose wrinkled, and gave them to her son, Carl. 'Take these out the back and burn them,' she said.

By the time they'd had a little food, it was evening. The girls climbed into bed in a haze of bewilderment and delight. It was such a long, long, almost forgotten time ago since they'd known anything like this. Clean bodies, clean hair, clean clothes, and soft, clean sheets. Pillows! *Pillows!!* Sheer, unbelievable bliss.

* * *

Bliss so pure rarely lasts long. In this case, it lasted until the middle of the night, when Friedel woke with a raging stomach ache. The discomfort she'd felt that morning was suddenly a horrible pain.

Maybe she'd eaten a bit too much, but she doubted it. Friedel still suspected it was the dodgy latkes they'd made in the camp the night before. She went off in urgent search of the toilet. For some reason it was in a sort of loft next to the kitchen, reached by a ladder.

Once she'd finished, she went back through the kitchen. She hadn't been gone very long, but to her astonishment the kitchen was suddenly full of soldiers, all talking in a foreign language. She recognised it as English.

Carl had been right. The Americans had arrived!

A couple of them tried talking to her, but Friedel struggled to understand. The English she'd learned from Mr Becker in Zbaszyn all those years ago had mostly been forgotten. But she remembered a little bit. Just enough to piece together what the Americans were saying, and soon she began to understand why they were here.

Their squad had been advancing along the road when they'd suddenly been fired at by German snipers hiding in a farmhouse nearby. One of the Americans described the house. It was the first house the girls had stopped at, the one that had given Friedel the creeps.

She'd felt as if it was watching her, and it had been. While she hesitated at the gate, a German sniper was probably looking at her through the sight of his rifle. She must have sensed it. A farmhouse filled with snipers waiting to ambush the enemy would have a stillness and silence about it that wasn't normal. What would have happened if she'd opened that gate? Would they have shot her? Captured her? It didn't bear thinking about.

By the next day, the American soldiers had dealt with the snipers and moved on, continuing their advance. Jeeps, trucks and tanks rumbled by, heading towards the main German front line a few kilometres up the road.

* * *

Mr Mayer, the farmer, turned out to be as kind as his wife. The twins were welcome to stay in the house for as long as they needed to, and to come and go as they pleased.

Perhaps the Mayers were so caring because they felt shame at what Germany had done to people like Friedel and Gina. Or maybe they were just kind people. More likely both those things were true.

The concentration camp at Turkheim still existed. The Americans had taken it over, and an outdoor kitchen had been set up there, serving food. With nowhere else to go, many of the prisoners who'd managed to escape into the countryside had returned to live in the camp for the time being. Those like Friedel and Gina who'd found places to stay were allowed to come there for hot food and a ration of milk. The food wasn't very good, admittedly, and there wasn't much more of it than the Germans had given them, but it was something.

For several days after that first night, Friedel had been too ill to go out, and so Gina had gone alone to fetch their ration. But eventually Friedel regained a little strength and decided to make the journey herself.

On this particular day, Gina was busy with something else – or just fed up with seeing the camp and its hideous memories. Friedel went with Franka instead.

(Mrs Mayer had been right. The four friends she'd had to turn away found places to stay nearby. It seemed that many of the folk of Turkheim were keen to repair the damage their fellow Germans had done. Most days the friends would get together in Friedel and Gina's room.)

It was a beautiful May day, warm and bright and cheerful, just over two weeks since their escape from the Death March. The war in Europe was over at last. Hitler had given up on his evil plans and had killed himself, just as the Russian troops were closing in on his underground bunker. Then, three days ago, on 8 May 1945, the Germans surrendered. All that fighting, all the death, all the suffering, all for nothing. Just for the sake of following the evil dreams of a group of hateful people.

The road to the camp passed through the village. It was a pleasant place. Not the most picturesque village in Bavaria by any means, but nice enough. There was a kind of square in the middle – really more of a big junction of main streets than a proper open space. It was surrounded by handsome buildings and a fine church, all painted white. In many Bavarian towns you'd see houses in all sorts of pretty colours, but in this area they seemed to like everything to be snow-white.

There was a bar in the square – the kind that Germans call a *Weinstube*, serving mainly wine and food. It wasn't serving anything at the moment, because the American army had turned it into accommodation for soldiers. A small group of Americans were sitting out in front having their hair cut.

As Friedel and Franka walked by, the soldiers smiled and said hello. The girls were intrigued by the strange, exotic-seeming men, and were happy to stop and chat. Or to chat as best they could. The soldiers were charming, and always keen to have female company. But they didn't talk to the camp survivors the way they might to local German women. It was more the way you might talk to lost children – concerned, caring. There was a name for the survivors: *KZ-lings*. KZ was short for *Konzentrationslager*, the German word for *concentration camp*. Everyone in Germany was learning to recognise when somebody was a KZ-ling. You could hardly mistake them, they were so thin and sick-looking.

There was one soldier who caught Friedel's eye. He stood out from the group. Tall, with dark hair and chiselled features, he was as handsome as a movie star. He gave both Friedel and Franka a dazzling smile.

'Hi, girls, my name's James. James Bilotta, from Massachusetts. You can call me Jimmie.' Seeing their blank looks, he pointed to himself and said, 'Me, Jimmie.' He pointed to another soldier who'd stood up with him. 'This is my pal, Bowman. Say hi, Bowman.'

The soldier smiled. 'At your service, girls.'

Friedel answered slowly in broken English. 'I am Friedel. Mine, my er, friend . . . has name Franka.'

Jimmie gazed at them for a moment. His smile faltered a little, giving way to pity. It was just as well

the girls couldn't see themselves through his eyes. To him, they looked so starved they were like bundles of sticks wrapped up in rags. Their faces were so hollowed out that their eyes were like great gleaming saucers. They were so thin and looked so small that Jimmie took them for kids. Maybe fifteen years old at most, he guessed. It wrung his heart to see children in such a state.

'Where are you girls living?' he asked.

Once she'd managed to grasp what he meant, Friedel told him the address of the Mayer farmhouse. Jimmie couldn't understand a word she was saying, so she picked up a stick and scratched the address in a patch of dust at the roadside.

Jimmie grinned. 'Now, *that* I can understand.' He dug in his uniform pocket and pulled out a handful of American chocolate bars. They were in brown wrappers with lots of official-looking writing on them. 'Army-issue,' he explained, seeing how bewildered the girls were. 'Go on, take 'em. They're better than they look. I'd give you some soap and stuff but we're fresh out.'

Bowman laughed. 'Jimmie's handed out half our regiment's PX stock to the kids round here. Not to mention our rations. We got nothing left over for us!'

Friedel and Franka had no idea what any of this meant. But they took the chocolate gratefully.

'Now, you take care, girls, OK?' With a last movie-star smile from Jimmie, Friedel and Franka went on their way.

* * *

Later that afternoon, Friedel, Gina and Franka were in their room, lounging on the bed, and on a mattress on the floor. Suddenly there was a creak of floorboards on the landing followed by a rap of knuckles on the door.

'Come in,' said Gina.

It opened, and a familiar face peeked in. 'Hi girls, it's us, we've come a-calling. Your landlady let us in.'

Friedel jumped up eagerly. 'Jimmie! Come in, come in.'

He stepped inside the room, followed by his friend Bowman. 'We come bearing a cornucopia of gifts,' said Jimmie. 'Look what we managed to rustle up! Put 'em down right there, Bowman.'

The two soldiers placed a stack of chocolate bars on the table, along with some bars of American soap.

'Thank you,' said Friedel, her eyes glowing. 'Is very . . . *kind*? Yes, kind.'

'You're more than welcome, young lady.'

With difficulty, Friedel introduced her twin sister. She'd already told Gina the thrilling story of the two Americans she'd met.

Gina picked up one of the soap bars. It was wrapped in crinkly lime-green paper with a black band round it, marked with the name *Palmolive*. Gina held it to her nose and closed her eyes in delight. 'Oh my god, Friedel, smell this!'

They hadn't had perfumed soap in years – hardly any soap at all, for that matter. The rough 'war soap' at Mrs Mayer's had been welcome enough, but this American stuff was incredible. Gina tore off the paper and fondled the yellow, waxy bar of soap inside. It was like handling some precious gem stolen from a sultan's treasure-house.

The girls chattered delightedly to each other in Polish, confident that the Americans wouldn't be able to understand a word.

'He's quite cute, isn't he?' said Franka.

Gina glanced at the soldiers. 'Which one?'

'The dark one, of course. Friedel fancies him, I'm sure.'

'Shut up!' said Friedel, glancing at Jimmie in alarm, as if he might hear. She realised that Bowman was listening to their conversation with a smile.

Jimmie caught the look, and grinned. 'You oughta know that Bowman's folks are Polish immigrants,' he said. 'He can understand every word you're saying. Can't you, pal?' To Friedel's horror, Bowman nodded, with a grin. Jimmie nudged him. 'So what're they saying?'

'Well, this young lady,' Bowman said, nodding towards Friedel, 'thinks you're kinda funny looking. What was it you said? *Big nose and head like a turnip?*'

Friedel went bright red. 'No! I did *not* say that!'

She looked at Jimmie, aghast, but he just burst out laughing. 'Bowman's a kidder,' he said.

Gina and Franka joined in the laughter, and eventually so did Friedel. It felt good. Laughter – real, heartfelt laughter – was another forgotten pleasure.

'We have had no meal yet,' said Gina once it died down. Her English was far better than Friedel's – her Zbaszyn lessons hadn't faded away, it seemed. 'Will you eat with us?'

The two Americans were embarrassed. 'We don't want to intrude,' said Jimmie. He knew how little the survivors got to eat, and didn't like to make it any less.

'Oh, please eat,' said Friedel. 'Is enough for you also.'

The girls brought out what they had, a mixture of rations from the camp kitchen and a little given by Mrs Mayer. It wasn't much. Black bread with some cream cheese, some potato soup with a little meat in it, and a canister of milk, which was starting to turn sour.

After dinner, Bowman took a harmonica from his pocket. He had carried it everywhere with him, all the way from the United States and through every battle he'd been in. He began to play a popular tune from back home.

Gina was delighted by this. When the tune was finished, she asked excitedly, 'Can I? I play a little.'

Bowman wiped the harmonica on his sleeve and handed it to her. She put it to her lips. To the astonishment of the Americans, she played with fantastic skill. Even more surprisingly, the first tune she played was the 'Horst Wessel Song', which had been the national anthem of Nazi Germany. Everyone in Germany knew it well, and it was as if, for Gina and the other girls, the stirring tune was somehow separate from its nasty meaning. Friedel and Franka hummed along and even sang some of the words.

Next Gina played a fast, jovial tune that she said was called 'Rosamunda'.

'Hey,' said Bowman. 'That's the "Beer Barrel Polka"!'

While Gina played and tapped her foot in time, the Americans sang the English words and Friedel sang the German version.

The music went on. There were German songs and traditional Jewish ones. And when they weren't singing, they were talking in a mixture of English, German and Polish, with a lot of translating and sign language.

Through the conversations, Jimmie realised that the girls were not children after all, not even teenagers. They were grown-up women in their twenties. It made him think all over again of what a terrible experience they'd been through, for it to have done this to them.

And his heart swelled with admiration for the courage they showed, and how they were able to laugh and sing in spite of it all.

Before they knew it, evening was starting to creep up on them. Jimmie and Bowman had to get back to their regiment. They said goodnight and left the girls in a haze of contentment.

Friedel, Gina and Franka hadn't known happiness this rich for . . . oh, they couldn't even remember. Maybe they'd never had an evening quite as blissful as this one. It was just what they'd needed.

CHAPTER NINETEEN

The Way Home

Jimmie Bilotta's war had been a tough one. He'd been sent over from America in December 1944, and was launched straight into the fighting with his regiment. Since then he'd been in many battles, large and small, and many friends of his had died. But now it was all over, and he felt triumphant. He felt that the world was free at last, and was proud that he'd helped to make it happen. But he also felt that he needed to do more.

Jimmie had given himself a new mission. He saw the Jews of Europe as America's allies in the war against Nazism. Now that the Nazis were destroyed, Jimmie needed to help those allies. And so he made it his quest to help Friedel and Gina get well again. He wanted to aid their friends, too, but it was the twins who had captured most of his heart.

The day after their magical first evening, Jimmie went shopping. First he tracked down a nearby music shop and bought three brand-new harmonicas for Gina – each one in a different key so that she could play a variety of tunes.

Then he went looking for one of the traders who dealt in food. With the country in chaos, supplies were difficult to get, and the black market was thriving. Jimmie's pockets were filled with packets of cigarettes. Because so many people smoked in those days, the army issued soldiers with free cigarettes. On the German black market cigarettes were so prized that they were like money. Jimmie didn't smoke, so he used all his supply to trade for food. One cigarette bought one fresh egg. A few more could buy you a good steak. After buying the makings of a good dinner, Jimmie stopped at the bakery and traded some chocolate for a fresh loaf of bread.

Laden with all these treasures, he headed to the Mayer farmhouse. Friedel and Gina were dumbstruck when he strode in and laid it all on the table.

Within minutes, Mrs Mayer had been called in and agreed to help cook the food. Soon the steaks and eggs were frying on her stove, filling the kitchen with delicious aromas. Jimmie sat at the table while the cooking was going on, and then watched happily as the twins and their friends devoured the meal.

For Jimmie, it felt as if he was coming back to life. Battles and grief had left him dazed. Now, seeing these poor survivors enjoying themselves and eating good, healthy food, all because of him ... well, it was the most beautiful thing in the world, greater than any riches.

Over the weeks and months that followed, Friedel and Gina slowly put on weight. Their limbs fleshed out and their bellies, which had been swollen by starvation, returned to normal. Their cheeks lost the sunken hollows, and they became what they truly were – beautiful young women.

As time went by, it was Friedel that Jimmie began to focus on. He adored Gina too, but with Friedel he felt a special bond. When Jimmie's regiment was ordered to move from Turkheim to another part of Germany, they held a big dance at the wine bar for all the soldiers and their friends (and their dates, if they had them). Jimmie, of course, took Friedel.

She had the time of her life. They drank wine and beer and danced all evening to the intense, thrilling sounds of American jazz. Afterwards, they took a long walk down by the river, where the sycamore branches dipped down to the still water, gleaming in the moonlight. And there they kissed.

It was beautiful. It was simple. They were in love.

* * *

Friedel lay on her bed, daydreaming. Mostly about Jimmie. His regiment had moved away, but he came

back to visit whenever he got the chance. The world was changing around her, and she was changing with it. Seven years had passed since the Nazis had forced her family out of their home, out of Germany. She could never have imagined then where that dreadful journey would take her. And she would certainly never have guessed where it would lead her in the end.

During the bitterest days in the ghetto and the camps, it had seemed that all their lives would be short and filled with misery. Only the luckiest and the most determined had survived. And now, by and by, their lives were their own again. So long as luck stayed with them, that is.

For many, it did not. The Allies were failing to provide enough help for the thousands upon thousands of concentration camp survivors. With all the people who had been in other kinds of Nazi camps – such as the forced labour camps, where people from conquered lands were brought to work – the survivors numbered millions. There wasn't enough food, shelter or medical care to go around. Some people were suffering almost as badly as they had in the camps. Since escaping from the Death March, Friedel and Gina had been incredibly courageous, incredibly strong, but also unbelievably lucky.

While Friedel was busy falling in love, Gina had also been making exciting plans for her future. She'd made a new friend among the survivors, a Jewish girl named Daniela, from Romania. Daniela had managed to get all the documents and money she needed to go back to her own country. She'd asked Gina to go with her, to try to make a new life in Romania. Without really thinking it through, Gina had leapt at the chance. The arrangements were made quickly, and this morning Gina and Daniela had left for the train station.

The goodbyes between Friedel and her twin had been hard to bear, with hugs and floods of tears. It broke Friedel's heart to see Gina go. If she hadn't had Jimmie in her life, she couldn't have borne it. But at least Gina had a chance to make a new life, and if she was lucky, perhaps it would be a happy one. Friedel had little idea what Romania was like. It had been taken over by the Nazis during the war, and most of its Jewish people had died in the Holocaust. Daniela wasn't likely to find any of her family still there when she returned.

There was a knock on the bedroom door. Mrs Mayer's son, Carl, came in and said, 'You've got a visitor downstairs.'

Friedel sat up. 'A visitor?' Her first thought was that it would be Jimmie, but he usually came straight up. 'Who is it?'

'An English soldier,' said Carl. 'Says he's your brother.'

Friedel's mind was blank. Surely the boy was joking with her. For one thing, there weren't any British troops in this area. For another, why would one of them claim to be her brother?

'You're trying to trick me, aren't you?'

Carl shook his head. 'Says he's your brother. Come down if you don't believe me.'

Bewildered, Friedel followed Carl downstairs to the kitchen.

A British soldier was standing near the window. He looked at her as she came in. Friedel peered curiously back at him. Well, he was a British soldier all right, with sergeant's stripes on his sleeve. He was studying her as intently as she was studying him. There was something familiar about him – rather handsome, with dark, gentle eyes and an easy smile. Then it struck her, and she gasped.

She saw the same face: younger, smoother, smiling across the dinner table in the apartment in Dusseldorf. All the years, the heartache, the grief, came bubbling up inside Friedel, bursting out of her in a scream.

'*MAX!*' Friedel flew across the room, and flung her arms round her brother. 'Max! Oh my god, Max!'

'It really is you!' he said, laughing. 'I wasn't sure if I should believe it. Good god, Friedel, it's really you!'

They both wept for joy and hugged again. Max held her at arm's length and studied her.

'Friedel, you're a grown woman now. I can hardly believe it!'

Once they'd calmed down, they sat at the table. There was so much to tell. On Max's side it was all good, but on Friedel's it was terrible, almost too terrible to even say. The loss, the heartbreak. Father's death. Mum taken away and gone forever. Bernard taken, and most likely dead too. Hans vanished.

'But tell me about England, Max,' Friedel said. 'How are you? How's Martha? Is she all right?'

'Oh, she's doing very well. Believe it or not, she got married three years ago, to an Englishman. They've just had a little baby girl. Can you imagine our Martha with a husband and a kid? As for me, well you can see, I'm a soldier now, in the British army. Well, the Free Polish Army really, but at the moment that's pretty much the same thing. We're under British command, and they provide all our gear.'

'So I see. It suits you! But Max, how on earth did you even know I was here?'

'Well, you know they put up lists of all the survivors who've been registered with the Allied authorities? I've been searching every day, hoping some of our family would still be alive. I didn't have much hope. I've been back to Dusseldorf. A couple of our relatives have made it back, happily, but that's all. And then I saw your and Gina's names on the list. As soon as I got leave to travel, I came to find you.' Max looked around. 'Is Gina here? I can't wait to see her.'

'Not right now, she ...' Friedel's smile froze on her face. 'Oh Max, she left for the station earlier! She's going to Romania!'

* * *

Gina and Daniela sat on a bench on the platform, waiting. The train services were almost as ramshackle as they'd been during the war. Unsurprisingly, their train was late. Gina hated the waiting – she wanted to get going. She was excited at the thought of the journey, and of the new life that might be waiting for her.

Itching with eagerness, she couldn't sit doing nothing. She got up and paced the platform. Walking back and forth aimlessly, her thoughts elsewhere, she found herself near the noticeboard. A sheaf of papers was pinned to it – the latest lists of survivors. 'Displaced persons' they were called.

She and Friedel were displaced persons, as were all their friends. People with no homes, and in many cases no countries. Although Gina and Friedel were German by birth and Polish by ancestry, they didn't belong to either of those countries any more. The Nazis had taken away their right to be German, and the Polish government had never accepted them. They were what the Germans called *Staatenlos*: stateless. That meant they had no nationality. Hundreds of thousands of other people were in the same limbo. While many survivors of the Holocaust, like Daniela, were making their way home, the stateless had nowhere to return to. For Gina, then, Romania made as much sense as anywhere else.

She leafed idly through the list on the noticeboard. The names flickered by in a blur. So many of them. Each one a life, each one mourning the dear ones who hadn't made it.

Suddenly Gina went rigid. A name leapt out from the list at her. She blinked and looked again . . .

Then she turned and started to run.

* * *

Max and Friedel were distraught. If only Gina hadn't gone off in such a rush! If only Max had managed to get here a day earlier. But there was nothing to be done. Gina was long gone. Would they even be able to find her again in all the chaos?

They were trying to rally their spirits when they heard the front gate clatter and the sound of footsteps running towards the kitchen door. A familiar voice was crying out, 'Friedel! Friedel!'

The door opened, and Gina burst into the room, gasping for breath. 'Friedel, he's alive! He's *alive*!'

Friedel jumped up and rushed to her, her words tumbling out as frantically as her sister's. 'Gina! Who's alive? What happened to Romania? Look, Max is here!'

'He's alive, Friedel – Bernard. Bernard's alive! I saw his name!'

Gina caught sight of the British soldier standing by the table, and she stopped talking. He looked familiar. The name Friedel had just mentioned, which was clunking around in her mind, suddenly connected with the face in front of her.

'Max!'

She almost fainted with shock. This was beyond belief! To have lost everyone they loved, then to find two dear brothers in one day! It was more joy than a person could bear.

Once Gina had calmed down and had caught up with all Max's news, she described what she'd seen on the list. *Bernard Rosenthal.* It was their Bernard, she was sure. The date of birth matched. And it said he was in Dusseldorf! As soon as he'd found freedom, Bernard must have had the same instinct as Max – to head for their old home in search of other survivors.

They all knew what they had to do now. Max, Gina and Friedel had to go to Dusseldorf too. They had to find Bernard.

* * *

Another heartbreaking goodbye, but bittersweet this time.

'I have to go, Jimmie,' said Friedel. 'You know that.'

'Of course,' he said. 'I understand. But I can't bear to let go of you.'

It was tearing Friedel in two as well. 'I wish I could stay, but I have to go.'

'Just tell me you won't forget me.'

Friedel put her arms round Jimmie and kissed him. 'I won't forget you. How could I ever do that? I want to be with you forever. This will just be for a short while.'

Jimmie's heart ached. His duties with the army kept him tied to one place. He couldn't go with her, and might not even be able to travel to visit her, so far away.

'We'll meet again one day,' he said. 'In England, maybe. It'll be safe for you there. Go find your brother. I'll come and find you as soon as I can.'

'And we'll be married.'

'We will. If you'll have me, I'll be the best husband you could ever wish for. We'll meet up in England, and then we'll go live in America. You'll love it there.'

With a parting kiss from Jimmie, Friedel set off with Gina and Max to search for their brother. Going to Dusseldorf should have felt like going home, even if home was a smouldering pile of rubble. But it wasn't their home any more. Nowhere was.

For Friedel, from now on home would be wherever Jimmie was. And it would be a good home, the best home. They would make their own life in America, far from the memories of the war and the Nazis, the ghetto and the camps. That was all past now. The future lay ahead of them, and it was beautiful.

What Happened After

At the beginning of this book, I set out to tell a story, and you set out to read it. All stories have an ending, and we have reached the end of this one, with Friedel and Gina heading back to Dusseldorf with their brother, Max, to find Bernard.

If this were a made-up tale, we could leave it there, and your imagination could fill in the rest. You could make up your own happy-ever-after for Friedel and Jimmie. But this isn't a made-up tale. It happened in real life. Gina and Friedel were real people, who lived this story, and real people go on living long after the stories we tell about them have ended. Naturally, you would probably like to know how their life stories went on.

What happened after the last full stop of the last chapter?

Well, Friedel, Gina and Max were reunited with Bernard in Dusseldorf. It was very strange to be back in the place where it had all begun. They were different people now, changed by all they had been through. The old city was no longer home for any of them, and never would be. They didn't stay for long.

Friedel and Jimmie did eventually get married, but it wasn't as easy as they'd hoped. Their dream of going to live in America didn't come true. The Allied countries set up a kind of government to run Germany. With the war over, Jimmie left the army and worked for this government. It upset him greatly that survivors of the Holocaust were being treated poorly, with hardly any of the help they needed. And it made him angry that people who were known to be Nazi war criminals were being let off without punishment. Some were even given good jobs in the government.

Jimmie wrote about what he'd seen for his local newspaper back in America. The things he described made the American government look bad, and they were embarrassed and angry. Their special crime investigation force, the FBI, investigated Jimmie, trying to find out anything bad he might have done, so that they could blacken his name and cast doubt on what he'd written. They did the same to Friedel, making up lies about both of them. As a result, Jimmie wasn't allowed to bring Friedel with him to America. He wrote to the newspapers about it, and published a short book telling the story of what Friedel had been through at the hands of the Nazis. There was sympathy from the American public, but the government didn't care.

With America ruled out, Friedel went to join Martha in England. Eventually Jimmie gave up trying to reason with the American government. He came and joined Friedel in England.

After they were married, they settled down in London. They had a daughter, Valerie, who'd been born in Germany while Friedel was still living as a displaced person. Later they had two more children, both boys.

Gina gave up her plan to move to Romania, and instead came to live in England too. She trained as a nurse, and then got married and had a baby daughter, named Wendy.

In the 1960s, in her typically adventurous way, Gina upped sticks and moved with her husband and daughter to America, where they settled in Baltimore. Brother Max was already living there, which was part of Gina's reason for moving. Max loved having at least some of his family near him.

Bernard, meanwhile, had gone to live in Israel, which had become an official country shortly after the war. He became much more involved with his Jewishness, he and his wife raising their children in the faith. He'd come a long way since he was a boy, when he'd spent the money given to him for his bar mitzvah lessons on sweets. He'd been through experiences just as terrible as Friedel and Gina had, mainly in the notorious Buchenwald concentration camp. All survivors were changed by the

Holocaust. Many lost their belief in God altogether, but some, like Bernard, believed more strongly.

One way or another, all the Rosenthal children made lives for themselves in the aftermath of the war and the Holocaust – except Hans. His visit to the family in Zbaszyn in 1939 was the last they ever saw of him, and his letters from Mogilev were the last news they ever received. After the war, his siblings tried to find out what had become of him. They asked the British Red Cross to help, but the investigation found no trace. The fate of Hans remains a mystery to this day. It is possible that he and his wife survived and lived on in Russia. But more likely, they were victims of the same evil as so many others. When the German forces captured the city of Mogilev in 1941, the Jews living there were swept into the Nazi system. Most were killed.

In 1991, Friedel had a phone call from Bernard. He told her that Gina was terribly ill in hospital, and desperately wanted to see her twin.

For over twenty years, with Gina living on the far side of the world, Friedel had felt as if a part of herself was missing. The three sisters visited each other from time to time, but Friedel still missed her twin painfully. There was nothing for it – she had to go and be with her, right away. But it was difficult. Jimmie was also ill and needed looking after constantly. Martha and her family agreed to take care of him for a while, and

Friedel rushed to America. She arrived on her and Gina's birthday, 24 January. They were both sixty-seven years old now.

As soon as Friedel saw her twin, she knew it was the last birthday they would share. Gina had leukaemia, and there was no hope of her getting better. Seeing her in a hospital bed, weak and close to death, for Friedel it was like being back in Turkheim again, in the hell of the typhus pit. She yearned to save her sister, as she had back then. She longed to take her out of this place and bring her home.

'You'll get better,' she told her. 'I promise. You'll get better and go home.' But in her heart, Friedel felt it wasn't true.

It tore Friedel to pieces that she couldn't stay longer. Jimmie needed her, and she had to leave.

Jimmie died in 1995. A few months later, at the suggestion of her family, Friedel agreed to tell the whole story of what had happened to her in the Holocaust. With great determination, she sat down and recorded an interview. It was painful for her, and it went on for hours. In it she traced her memories all the way back to Dusseldorf, telling the story that I have retold here.

Friedel herself died in 2002, aged seventy-eight. Her sister Martha died in 2005, aged eighty-five.

* * *

WHAT HAPPENED AFTER

In 2019, I published a book called *The Boy Who Followed His Father into Auschwitz*, which told a true story of people surviving the Holocaust.* It was a deeply moving story of courage and love. It touched everyone who read it.

Some wrote to tell me their own family's stories of the Holocaust. One of those people was Friedel's daughter, Valerie. She told me that her mother had been through the Holocaust, and that she had a remarkable story to tell. I talked to Valerie, and eventually also to Gina's and Martha's daughters. I realised that their mothers' experiences were as unusual and incredible as those recounted in my previous book. It felt natural to me that the story of two brothers – Fritz and Kurt Kleinmann – should be paired with a story of two sisters, Friedel and Gina Rosenthal.

The two stories go together, mirroring each other in many aspects. But they also show the different ways in which people were ensnared by the evils of Nazi Germany. The two books may cover the same years, but the range of experiences is very different in each.

This book is therefore dedicated to everyone who went through that terrible era, those who survived and those who did not. And it is for the descendants, especially the

---

* Later on I wrote a version of the story for young readers, titled *Fritz and Kurt*.

daughters of the three sisters – Friedel's daughter Valerie, Gina's daughter Wendy, and Martha's daughter Lynn.

And above all others, it is for the two amazing sisters themselves:

> Friedel Rosenthal, 1924–2002
> Gina Rosenthal, 1924–1991

Acknowledgements

I am grateful to all who have helped this book come to life.

My deepest gratitude is to the descendants of the Rosenthal family, who have entrusted me with their story, encouraged me and helped my research. Wendy Chmielewski (Gina's daughter) spent hours talking with me about her memories of her mother, and provided many useful notes on the manuscript. Lynn Reeves (Martha's daughter) was generous with her time and memories, and allowed me access to her excellent family archive of documents, recordings and photos. Above all I am profoundly grateful to Valerie Prestage (Friedel's daughter), who first brought her mother's story to my attention and shared with me her own memories along with Friedel's recorded recollections. Without Val, this book would not exist. Her role in encouraging her mother to record her story ensured that a truly extraordinary account of surviving the Holocaust has been preserved for the historical record.

ACKNOWLEDGEMENTS

Special thanks to my wonderful illustrator, Raquel Lagartos, whose ideas and sketches helped to inspire me while I was writing, and whose illustrations make this book so much better than it would otherwise have been.

The manuscript was read by historical consultants Hannah Randall and Dr Chelsea Sambells. Their notes have helped to correct and improve my text significantly. If any historical issues remain, they are entirely my fault.

Finally, my thanks go to my publishers. The time, care and attention to detail given to the manuscript by Tom Rawlinson at Puffin Books UK has been a boon and an inspiration. And as ever, I am grateful to my literary agent, Andrew Lownie, for his many years of patient support.

Jeremy Dronfield
February 2025

Friedel (right) and Gina on their first day of school.